W9-ADD-467

*UNDERSTANDING
THE BIBLE*

UNDERSTANDING THE BIBLE

Ignatius Hunt, O.S.B.

SHEED AND WARD · NEW YORK

© Sheed & Ward, Inc., 1962

Library of Congress Catalog Card Number 62–9109

220.1
Hu

IMPRIMI POTEST:

✠ ANSELM COPPERSMITH, O.S.B.
Abbot of Conception Abbey
Conception, Missouri
DECEMBER 1, 1961

NIHIL OBSTAT:

JOHN R. READY
Censor Librorum
NOVEMBER 28, 1961

IMPRIMATUR:

✠ ROBERT F. JOYCE
Bishop of Burlington
DECEMBER 1, 1961

MANUFACTURED IN THE UNITED STATES OF AMERICA

To my beloved mother and father

PREFACE

RECENT YEARS have seen a number of attempts at popularizing the vast scholarly work that is now being carried on in the biblical field. It is our conviction that there is room for many popularizations of this kind as long as they are presented in a solid and accurate manner. Whether this book belongs to this class is for others to judge. Its chief merits, if we may speak of them, are those of attempting to show the scientific necessity for the new era in biblical science; the guidance which the Holy See has given to this work; and some practical applications. In an Introduction and twenty-seven chapters we have attempted to cover an admittedly broad area. The work is not intended for specialists (who would have little to learn from it), but for priests, religious, and faithful who are interested either in having a quick review of a subject with which they are already generally familiar or in getting a short introduction to present-day biblical studies. We have attempted to avoid terms that would only puzzle our intended reading audience, and where this was not possible we have made an effort to define the terms.

Biblical citations are often our own translation; frequently they are taken from the Knox version; and at times from other versions. Where no acknowledgement is made the citation will be our own.

Needless to say, this book is not original. It depends on the pioneering work of many great scholars and is no more than an abbreviated compilation of their study.

The author wishes to thank his superiors who have afforded

him the time and means for the pursuit of biblical studies as well
as Sheed and Ward, publishers, for their great kindness and
understanding in working out details of this book.

Rome, Pontifical Biblical Institute,

IGNATIUS HUNT, O.S.B.

Feast of St. Jerome, September 30, 1961

CONTENTS

INTRODUCTION: A NEW ERA
IN BIBLICAL STUDIES

No LESS AN AUTHORITY than the late Pius XII, in the opening pages of his epoch-making 1943 encyclical (*On the Most Opportune Way to Promote Biblical Studies*),[1] stated that "there is no one who cannot easily perceive that the conditions of biblical studies and their subsidiary sciences *have greatly changed within the last fifty years.*" That was almost nineteen years ago, for the encyclical bears the date of September 30, 1943.

Changes present problems and are not generally easy to face. Yet it is only by acquainting ourselves with changes and the reasons that underlie them that we can genuinely serve the Church. This is true in any field—including that of the Bible.

It is our purpose to discuss primarily the "greatly changed conditions" of biblical studies, spoken of by Pius XII; and by discussing them to provide for a more fruitful and intelligent use of Sacred Scripture, in keeping with the *express* wishes of the Holy See, which alone is the final and infallible interpreter of the Bible.

The Bible is an eternal, divinely inspired *library* of books that "have God for their author" (Vatican Council, DB *Enchiridion Symbolorum*, No. 1787); no less is the Bible a temporal, human collection of writings, for while every word of the inspired text, as we shall see, comes from God, just as surely does every word come from and through *men*.

The whole background against which the Bible was *humanly*

[1] In *Rome and the Study of Scripture* (St. Meinrad, Indiana; Grail Publications, 6th ed., 1958), pp. 80–107.

written has, in recent years, taken on a clarity that it never had before, especially when we consider that for long centuries the Bible itself was almost the only criterion by which to evaluate the events it relates. This clarity has come to us through vast archaeological discoveries made throughout the Near East during the past century; through the unearthing of entire libraries of ancient literatures; through an ever surer knowledge of the Semitic tongues and the philosophy that lies behind them, and, the crowning achievement, through giant strides made in our understanding of the "manner of speaking, relating, and writing in use among the ancients" (Pius XII). We have learned to go back "wholly in spirit to those remote ages of the East" and enter into their way of thinking, conceiving, and recording. This means that the present-day expositor of the Bible can go about his task of determining *what the Bible means* (its "literal sense") with a guidance and assurance that his predecessors simply did not have.

Let us not think that the implementation of all this information has come about with ease and harmony—for such is not the case. To revamp one's outlook is at times difficult, even painful, and this is true of the matter at hand. As archaeological evidence and ancient documents were brought into the world of biblical studies, and especially as some of this material was used by non-believers or liberals to discredit the Bible, Catholic authorities and scholars alike became sharply divided in their views. Not a few sincere men met the strongest opposition from other equally sincere men when they attempted to make an objective and scholarly use of archaeological discoveries.

The pioneer in this huge work of synthesis was Père Marie-Joseph Lagrange, O.P., who founded in 1890 the famous Ecole Biblique et Archeologique in Jerusalem. It was this man, at once a thorough scholar and an unflinchingly loyal son of the Church, who foresaw that the only possible course was to neglect *nothing* that might clarify the meaning of the Bible, to have faith enough in the inspired Word of God to study it with complete objectivity and scientific honesty, and to meet the opponents of the Bible on their own ground. Though Lagrange was suspected and accused by a number of his contemporaries, he stood his ground, keeping in close contact with Rome, and it is precisely his policy that the Church has made her own—first through the 1893 encyclical of Leo XIII (*The Most Provident God*), and, fifty years later, with greater clarity and force, through Pius XII, whose biblical encyclical is, among other things, a complete vindication of this "greatest benefactor of Catholic exegesis."

The policy that the Holy See has adopted demands from her biblical scholars great labor, intellectual integrity, loyalty, and not a little faith. The exegete must grapple with the most fundamental problems of religion, must be absolutely objective in his search for truth, yet always a trusted son of the Church. Needless to say, not all measure up to these stern requirements—but they stand as a challenge to these men who have been set aside by their superiors to devote their lives to the study and explanation of Scripture.

On another point, too, the Roman directives are very clear; viz., that the *solid fruits* of biblical study are to be generously shared with priests, religious, seminarians, *and the faithful.* "So vast is the scope of biblical knowledge, *so many and so great are the advances* made in the explanation of the Sacred Books, so numerous are the sciences whose aid must be invoked that the professor, unless he devotes himself daily to diligent study, soon becomes unequal to this arduous office and is incapable of rendering the service which priests engaged in the ministry of souls and *even the faithful* rightly demand of him" (1950 *Instruction* of the Pontifical Biblical Commission).

Not infrequently have those trained in an earlier age shown surprise and shock at the conclusions (often tentative) of modern biblical science. Sometimes, of course, this is justified, for biblical scholars are not infallible and have on occasion drawn quite unwarranted conclusions from the evidence at hand. Yet Pius XII has a kind word for these men: "Let all other sons of the Church bear in mind that the efforts of these resolute laborers in the vineyard of the Lord should be judged not only with equity and justice, but also with the greatest charity. All, moreover, should abhor that intemperate zeal which imagines that whatever is new should for that very reason be opposed or suspected." The same pontiff pointed out that "there are *but few texts* whose sense has been defined by the authority of the Church, nor are those more numerous about which the teaching of the Holy Fathers is unanimous."

All this should make us realize that there is lots of room for biblical investigation and that, contrary to what some outside the Church think, Catholic scholars have a great amount of liberty in their work.

We may be thankful that the age (not so far back!) of a pre-dominantly *defensive,* almost fearful, study of the Bible has passed. This was a far cry from the vigorous and widespread use which the Church once made of the Bible in her catechetics, liturgy, and instruction. Many factors, such as Reformation polemics, accusations levelled against the Bible in the name of science, and Modernism, gradually made the Sacred Scriptures a closed and unknown book. Today we can once more build positively in a predominant atmosphere of joy and assurance. To Pius XII we owe an immense debt of gratitude for this healthy condition.

Readers interested in exploring these questions further will find Charles Hauret's *Beginnings: Genesis and Modern Science*[2] and Bruce Vawter's *The Bible in the Church*[3] most valuable books.

[2] Trans. and adapted by E. P. Emmans (Dubuque, Iowa; Priory Press, 1955).

[3] In Canterbury Books (New York, Sheed & Ward, 1950).

UNDERSTANDING
THE BIBLE

1 NEW TRENDS IN BIBLICAL INTERPRETATION

In 1941 a well-intentioned but badly misled Neapolitan priest (whose name was later divulged as Dolindo Ruotolo) sent a letter to pope, cardinals, archibishops, and bishops of Italy (simultaneously) in which he bitterly denounced the scientific study of the Bible as "a most grave danger" animated by an "accursed spirit of pride, presumption, and superficiality."

This letter in the same year provoked a lengthy reply from the Biblical Commission addressed to the Italian hierarchy. The reply outlined the various reasons *necessitating* a scientific study of the Bible, stating, in some detail, how this should be carried out.

Pius XII, as we have seen, clarified these same principles even further in 1943 through his famous encyclical, *On the Most Opportune Way to Promote Biblical Studies*. On May 13, 1950, the Biblical Commission reasserted these principles in an *Instruction* issued to ordinaries, religious superiors, seminary rectors, and Scripture professors throughout the Catholic world.

The *principles*, therefore, governing present-day biblical studies in the Church have been amply outlined and sanctioned by the Holy See. Their application to specific instances is left, in large part, to the judgment of Catholic scholars until some further declaration is made by the teaching authority of the Church. There is no doubt of the fact—the Church wants her scholars to investigate biblical questions and to bring out in print the fruits of their research. Let us take a look at some of the *broad lines* of present-day interpretation as well as some specific applications of them.

It is a *first principle* of *any* literary study to make every effort to capture the authentic meaning of the author. This principle is of special importance since there are many ways of writing up an account or of treating a subject—e.g., poetry, epic, satire, cold factual evaluation, comedy, fiction, parable. Everything that is written is written according to *some* "literary form"—a way of thinking, conceiving, and writing. This applies to the Bible as much as to any other literature (even though God is its principal author), and Pius XII is emphatic on the point: "The investigation, carried out during the past forty or fifty years with greater care and diligence than ever before, has more clearly shown what forms of expression were used in those far-off times, whether in poetic description or in the formulation of laws and rules of life or *in recording the facts and events of history*." Further on (in the same encyclical) he says: "Of the modes of expression which, among ancient peoples, and especially those of the East, human language used to express its thought, *none is excluded* from the Sacred Books, provided the way of speaking adopted in no wise contradicts the holiness and truth of God."

This approach through "literary forms" is of paramount importance and has reopened countless biblical discussions. Already in 1935, Augustine Cardinal Bea, S.J., at that time Rector of the Pontifical Biblical Institute in Rome, made the observation that "each literary form has its own truth." In practical terms, this means that such a biblical account as the famous sun incident in Joshua 10,[1] presented as it is in an epical-poetical literary setting, is probably no more than the recording of an hyperbolized story and not an historical assertion after *our* manner

---

[1] Joshua, i.e. Douay Josue. Here and elsewhere throughout the book the standard English spellings (which are found in most dictionaries and encyclopedias) are used. For a list with the Douay equivalents, please consult the Index of Scripture Texts.

of writing history. Again, for reasons that we shall discuss in greater detail, the long years assigned to the pre- and post-flood patriarchs have values other than our present-day notion of years and life-spans. Countless other conclusions, really startling at first encounter, have been reached by biblical scholars of our times: e.g. that Cain and Abel are *not* the *immediate* sons of First Man and First Woman; that the flood did *not* cover the entire universe or destroy all but eight men; that God did *not* actually communicate directly with men *every* time that the Bible states: "And the Lord said"; that a great many of the numbers in the Bible are inflated, and so on. We state these conclusions (and they could be extended at great length) not to appear revolutionary but merely to give an idea of what the application of the principles of literary forms signifies.

Much has been written in the papal documents about the *notion of history* in the ancient world. In principle, the directives are evident and common-sense; in practice, they result in some surprising conclusions. First, note what Pius XII said about history in the quotation given earlier. There is also a response of the Biblical Commission (January 16, 1948) to the late Cardinal-Archbishop of Paris, Emmanuel Suhard, in which it is said: "One can neither deny nor affirm the historicity [of the first eleven chapters of Genesis] taken as a whole, without unduly attributing to them the canons of a literary style within which it is *impossible* to classify them. If one agrees not to recognize in these chapters history in the *classical* and *modern* sense, one must, however, admit that the actual scientific data do not allow of giving all the problems they set a positive solution . . . one should examine closely the literary processes of the early Oriental peoples, their psychology, their way of expressing themselves and *their very notion of historical truth.*" In keeping with such directives, it is now held by most Catholic scholars that Judith, Tobit, and Esther have no more than a kernel of historical truth in them. The accounts given in these books are principally what might be called "didactic fiction." Nor need we think that this is contrary to earlier directives of the Biblical Commission, since the 1943 encyclical and the Suhard letter have implicitly reinterpreted the 1905 decree of the Pontifical Biblical Commission regarding portions of the Bible that only *appeared* to be historical.

Furthermore, few now regard the book of Jonah as historical. It is rather a clever piece of *satire* and instructive fiction pointing up the narrowness of post-exilic Judaism (represented by the person of Jonah) which didn't wish to share with other peoples the riches of its faith, and which even showed sorrow when others (represented by the Ninevites) manifested signs of good-will and penitence. This, at the same time, makes such standard problems as whether a whale can swallow a man without killing him vanish into thin air—as it should have done a long time ago.

Hebrew historians were simply different from modern historiographers. The Hebrews related incidents to bring out lessons, to illustrate religious doctrines, to show how God had intervened in their national life. The editor of Genesis, like the editors of other books of the Bible, did not hesitate to present two versions of the same story (creation, patriarchal listings, flood, etc.). The Hebrew storyteller was more interested in explaining "why" than in delineating "what really happened"—as strange as that may seem to us. The Hebrews were not abstract thinkers. They revelled in the concrete, the dynamic, the active. Such factors must be reckoned with if we are to understand the "salvation history" that we find in the Bible.

Very wisely, and only after sad experience, has Catholic biblical scholarship completely turned its back on "concordism"—the effort to make of the Bible a science manual, to work for "concord" between the Bible and every scientific theory. The Bible is simply not a scientific treatise, if we mean by that that it anticipated by hundreds of years modern scientific theory. The biblical writers were interested in religion, in the plan of salvation, and if they brought in anything which in our present way of thinking belongs to science, they brought it in under the *formal* aspect of religion. The Bible's conception of the universe was simply the common conception of the ancient Near East: a saucer-shaped earth, resting on pillars that sank way down in almost bottomless water; a solid, inverted bowl-like structure that stretched over the earth (the firmament), from which were suspended the celestial bodies and over which were stored vast quantities of water. The ancients had not arrived at an accurate understanding of the world, nor could they have done so.

Obviously, too, the six days of creation—an artificial device used to teach God's creatorship and the observance of Sabbath rest—are not to be drawn out into six geological periods of thousands of years each. Of this we shall see more later.

Archaeology, too, has thrown immense light on biblical interpretation. Thus we are enabled to date the exodus from Egypt with relative assurance at around 1275–1250 B.C. We have been able to situate the original city of Jerusalem (the Jebusite stronghold captured by David's forces). We have acquired an extensive knowledge of the completely polytheistic character of the Land of Canaan into which Abraham came as he journeyed from Ur and Haran. Every book of the Old Testament may now receive something of an archaeological commentary, as well as the theological commentary so strongly recommended by Pius XII— the theology thus being all the better grounded and solidified.

Modern scholars, too, are very hesitant about projecting back into the Old Testament doctrines which were only revealed in the New, such as Trinity, Divinity of Christ, Incarnation. It was "in many ways and by many means" (Heb 1, 1, Knox[2]) that God revealed his marvellous plan of redemption. To conceive of Adam as having understood the deepest mysteries of Christi-

[2] *The Holy Bible*, trans. Ronald Knox (New York, Sheed & Ward, 1950).

anity is an *opinion* to which few modern biblical scholars would care to sign their name.

The lesson in all of this is that we have to *take the Bible as it really is,* neither detracting from its genuine meaning nor injecting extraneous meanings into it. If modern biblical scholarship has arrived at conclusions foreign to past ages, it has done this only because the very kind of evidence respected and advocated in the papal documents has led it in this direction. We need have no fear that anything genuinely basic to Christianity is being destroyed.

2 *THE INSPIRATION OF SACRED SCRIPTURE*

THE BIBLE is different from all other books. What makes it different is not its majestic style (though some of its books are exceptionally well written), nor its capacity to engage our interest (for while some books have this ability, others make admittedly dull reading), nor its over-all elevation of thought (for some parts of the Bible have this quality while others are doctrinally weak and may even at times shock unprepared readers). The thing that makes the Bible unique is its *inspired character.* On this point the Catholic Church has never wavered. Biblical inspiration is a dogma of faith.

The term "inspiration" is itself biblical. St. Paul writing to his beloved disciple Timothy—both of them converts from Judaism and acquainted with the Hebrew Scriptures from their childhood—states (2 Tim 3, 16): "All Scripture [Paul is referring to the Old Testament books, and perhaps to those of the New Testament that were by this time recognized as Scripture] is divinely inspired. . . ." One Greek word, *theópneustos*, provides us with the translation "divinely inspired." This word means literally "breathed on by God," or "God-breathed." Paul's statement might be even better rendered: "All Scripture, divinely inspired, is useful. . . ." In either case the meaning of the expression is the same.

A similar idea is found in 2 Pet 1, 21 where the writer is dealing with biblical prophecy. He states that "it was never man's impulse, after all, that gave us prophecy; men gave it utterance, but they were men whom God had sanctified, carried away, as they spoke by the Holy Spirit" (Knox). The Latin Vulgate's translation of "carried away" is *inspirati* ("inspired"). The *idea* of men speaking or writing under divine impulse is frequently found in the Old Testament (cf. Jer 20, 7–9; Exod 17, 14).

The thought of Peter and Paul is that inspiration is an effect, produced by divine influence upon the writers of the Scriptures *as they are writing*.

St. Thomas Aquinas explained biblical inspiration through the notion of "instrumental causality." In the case of Sacred Scripture, God is the *principal cause* (comparable to a carpenter) who makes use of a man as his instrumental cause (comparable to the carpenter's tools) to produce the Sacred Writings. The effect is ascribed to *both* principal and instrumental causes, for one is not effective without the other. The tools cannot produce a table without the carpenter any more than the carpenter can produce the table without the tools.

There is, of course, one big difference, as Pius XII indicates, in the case of the Bible. The instruments that God uses are *living and reasonable agents*," each with his own character, abilities, and formation, so that the result will betray the instrument to no small degree. Thus one biblical writer is a clever gram-

marian and stylist (Isaiah), while another may actually be guilty
of solecisms and poor grammatical constructions (writer of the
Apocalypse). Obviously the biblical writers did not "pass out"
under divine influence and write in a merely mechanical, trance-
fashion. Thus, if we use the term "dictation" when speaking of
God's authorship of the Bible, as did the Council of Trent
("*Spiritu Sancto dictante*"), we must understand that this in no
way deprived the writers of consciousness, of freedom, of their
own peculiarities—for the Scriptures themselves give the lie to
such a viewpoint. It is precisely because God made use of *human* authors, who received their thoughts and notions in many
ways, that we must study the entire background of oriental
culture in order to evaluate correctly what the biblical writers
want to tell us. The Church, as we have seen, has definitely
taken a stand on this question.

Pope Leo XIII in his 1893 encyclical (*The Most Provident
God*) gave a classic definition of biblical inspiration. "By supernatural power," he says, "God so moved and impelled the human
authors to write, He so assisted them when writing, that the
things which He ordered, and those only, they first rightly understood, then willed faithfully to write down, and finally expressed in apt words and with infallible truth. Otherwise, it could
not be said that He was the Author of the entire Scripture." Inspiration is then a *process* (as well as an *effect*) involving the
human writer's intellect (speculative and practical judgment),
will, and faculties—all of which fall under the divine influence
in proportion to their function in a particular instance. The peak
of this process, says St. Thomas, is the *illumination of the speculative judgment,* which deals with truth, with "right understanding." The more lofty the matter at hand, the more potent must
this illumination be. For a psalmist to express his personal grief
does not require the illumination of mind that John needed in
thinking out the elevated doctrine contained in the Prologue

to his Gospel account. In *this sense,* we may speak of degrees of inspiration, even though all Scripture is inspired.

The practical judgment is also vital in the process, for it must decide *how* to express the truth at hand. Shall it be poetry, epic narrative, the language of theology, or hyperbole? Are previously existing documents to be used, and if so, are they to be used as such or should they be recast? In some instances the practical judgment needs more assistance than the speculative. In these intellectual steps, as well as in the movement upon will and faculties, God's influence is at work in the form of a special "charism" or grace granted to the sacred writer.

Did the sacred writers *realize* that they were writing under divine inspiration? In a few cases they may have been aware of this, but they need not have been, and it looks as if they actually were not so aware in *most* cases. Thus the writer of 2 Macc complains (2, 27) of the immense labor his condensation of the five books of Jason has cost him; Luke (1, 1-4) describes his research that led to the penning of the third Gospel; Paul wrote many of his letters to settle practical issues that arose in the churches he founded.

It is a matter of faith that *all* the Bible is inspired—that is, all those books declared by the Church to be canonical with all the parts that *originally* made them up. Glosses, textual inaccuracies, etc., do not fall under inspiration. Translations are *equivalently* inspired, *insofar as* they faithfully represent the original texts.

We may even say—in fact we must say—that *every word* of the Bible is inspired, for every word of the authentic Bible has come from the hand of an inspired writer. To assert that only those parts of Scripture that deal with "faith and morals" are inspired is an error already pointed out by Leo XIII in his 1893 encyclical. Inspiration must not be confused with revelation.[1]

---

[1] The term "revelation" is taken here in a strict sense. This term, as well as its relation to "inspiration," is the object of considerable study at the present time.

Only a small part of the Bible is actually revealed. Revelation is *not the same* as inspiration.

But *how* do we know that the Bible is inspired? What is the *criterion* of inspiration? Since inspiration is something *strictly supernatural, God alone* can inform us of the fact. Consequently, all purely natural criteria must be ruled out, such as the edifying character of the Bible (many other books are edifying, and some parts of the Bible are not), or Luther's famous "taste-test." We cannot appeal to Scripture itself, for the Bible never affirms inspiration for *all* that *now* makes up its contents. Too, it would be begging the question to ask Scripture to prove its own inspiration. The criterion that we seek must be *certain, universal,* and *accessible to all.* As Father Bruce Vawter, C.M., writes: "Since only God can testify to the fact, it follows that he must either make this knowledge available by personal revelation to every reader of the Scriptures—and this is empirically false and contrary to the teaching of Scripture itself—or he will provide it through the agency in whose teaching and practice his revelation is to be safeguarded, namely the Church."[2] The Church, then, is the only and ultimate criterion of biblical inspiration, even though her decision is based to some extent upon such tests as orthodox doctrine and apostolic authorship. She has voiced her final decision on this matter through the Councils of Florence, Trent, and the Vatican.

While recent Scripture research among Catholics has in no wise diminished the force of the traditional teaching on inspiration, it has raised a number of new questions and even invited fresh reflection on some secondary aspects of inspiration. This is only as it should be. Those who wish to see some of the finest efforts in this regard should consult the treatise on Inspiration in Volume I of the second English edition of *Guide to the Bible:*

[2] Unpublished class notes, General Introduction to Sacred Scripture, 1959–60. Very useful is Father Vawter's pamphlet *The Bible is Different* (Paterson, New Jersey; St. Anthony Guild Press, 1959).

an *Introduction to the Study of Holy Scripture,* by A. Robert and A. Tricot,[3] where Pierre Benoit, O.P., of the Ecole Biblique in Jerusalem, treats the subject exhaustively.

Needless to say, modern developments in our knowledge of *how* the books of the Bible were written (often in several stages, with various revisions, over a long period of time), demand that the charism of inspiration be *distributed* over the different writers, revisers, and editors, *in proportion to* their contribution towards the final product.

Yet Catholic dogma remains *essentially* the same: the entire Bible is inspired in all its authentic parts—even the individual words. This we call "total inspiration," the effect of a specific divine influence that makes the books of the biblical library unique.

3 *THE BIBLE, A LIBRARY OF ERRORLESS BOOKS*

"TO ERR IS HUMAN" runs the adage, and anyone laying claim to personal inerrancy would have to do a lot of explaining before a sensible man would accept his claim; and, of course, no sensible man, trusting in his own abilities, would dare make such a claim. This is one of the reasons why the definition of papal infallibility (wrongly understood) raised such storms of indignation from those who thought the Roman Pontiff was claiming personal infallibility and impeccability for his every statement and action.

[3] New York, Desclée, 1960.

For somewhat similar reasons, though the question is considerably more complex, the controversy that arose around the Catholic *dogma* of biblical inerrancy has been vast and heated. So pitched was the debate on this question during the nineteenth century that inerrancy became known as "THE biblical question." Just one biblical question was regarded as paramount: Does, or does not, the Bible contain error?

The Church's doctrine on inerrancy was formulated in an age when men, though assuredly noting many a biblical problem (largely through confronting one text with another), did not have to bear the brunt of assimilating the great mass of information that has come to light in our scientific age. Geology, anthropology, history, archaeology, comparative religion, and many other disciplines have risen up to challenge, or at least refocus, the doctrine on the Bible's inerrancy. Yet Catholic teaching remains essentially the same today as before. We need neither be ashamed of it nor disguise the issues it raises.

Inerrancy is simply a consequence (though not the only one!) of the Bible's inspired character. If God, who can neither deceive nor be deceived, is really the *principal author* of the Scriptures, then the idea is absolutely repugnant that his writings, even though he makes use of human instruments in their composition, should teach error in those matters which are their explicit and direct concern. To admit even one such error in the Bible would mean one too many as far as the Church's teaching is concerned.

But is this not placing the Catholic under an unjust and unreasonable strain? Our answer is: "No." Let us try to explain why.

First of all, inerrancy, like inspiration, is claimed only for the *original texts* of the Bible. If *any* version fails to convey the real meaning and spirit of the original text, this is the fault of the version and is no blemish on the Bible's inerrancy. The Latin Vulgate and its English counterpart, the Douay version, present a number of these inaccuracies. Thus in 1 Cor 15, 51, the negative particle has been misplaced, resulting in a glaring contradiction with the following verse. In verse 51 the Vulgate has Paul saying that "we shall not all be changed"; while in verse 52 it has him reversing his statement: "we shall all be changed." This contradiction is not found in the best Greek manuscripts, nor consequently in the critical Greek editions of the New Testament, nor should it, therefore, be found in *any* version.

"Error," too, is a concept that has been greatly refined in modern times. The ancients, though perceiving and understanding deception and mistakes, were not nearly so conscious of, or concerned about, absolute accuracy as we are today. This leads us once more into the ever important realm of the ancient "literary forms"—those ways of conceiving and writing prevalent in ancient times—often so different from our own. We must be on our guard about applying the modern concept of "error" to writers—in our case the human instruments of God—who simply did not share our sensitivity on many points of thinking and writing. It was not without good reason that St. Thomas Aquinas (*Summa Theologica,* 2a, 2ae, q. 173, a. 4) speaks of God's human instruments as "defective." For they had limited understanding, they found it hard to put across their message, and they had to express themselves as men of their times—the only way they could possibly have spoken.

Nor should we forget our own modern literary forms. Poets of today automatically receive a "license." The language of the beatniks is one with which few outsiders (including this writer) are entirely familiar. Epic writers are expected to glorify their hero. *Everything* we read is written according to some literary form.

Reducing all this to a principle, the Church's teaching on the inerrancy of the Bible refers to *formal error.* The Church teaches that there can be no lack of conformity between the sacred writer's *judgment* and the reality with which he is primarily concerned when he teaches—he makes no mistake in judging those objects which he intends to judge. Every statement intended by the sacred writer *as true* must be true in the way in which he intends it to be true (for no one can say everything at the same time), e.g. 1 Jn 5, 18— ". . . does not *go on* committing sin." It was precisely in making this judgment that the sacred writer was illuminated, not in others.

Thus the purpose of the "Priestly account" in Gen 1, 1 to 2, 4a in setting forth God's creative work in a six-day mould was not to teach that God actually created everything in six twenty-four-hour days, nor was it to teach that he created in six "periods" of thousands of years each (a concordistic explanation that is even further from the sacred writer's intention!), *but* to show that God is the maker of everything and that man should observe the Sabbath. The six twenty-four-hour days are an artificial device used by the writer to stress Sabbath observance. Other secondary purposes were also present, as we shall see; but to set forth a rigorously scientific account of how creation actually took place was obviously not the author's purpose, and hence does not fall under inerrancy in that way. We show fairness and reasonableness in judging modern writers. Is there any reason why this same fairness and reasonableness should not be shown to the biblical writers, who were no less human?

What we have in the Bible—and this is present in hundreds of instances—is *material error*: a lack of objective truth in some of the materials handled or presented. When the hare is enumerated among the animals that chew the cud (Lev 11, 6; Dt 14, 7), the modern reader rightly objects; but there is no formal error here, only material error. The writers of Leviticus and Deuteronomy were not scientific experts on natural history. Their interests here were ritualistic and Jewish. In the present context they simply followed a common belief of their time. The constantly twitching nose of the hare caused observers to believe that it was engaged in the process of chewing its cud. The sacred writers did not attempt a rebuttal of this viewpoint—if they so much as saw the need for such a rebuttal. They list the hare among the unclean animals because, according to ideas then current, the hare did not measure up to ritualistic purity standards.

We must not think that the Bible is constantly teaching, though it does this in one way or another much of the time. There are times when the Bible merely rouses us, consoles us, charms us, without formally instructing us—and it may instruct us in the most diverse manners. It is evident from 2 Tim 3, 16–17 that the Bible has various practical ends that may or may not accompany instruction: "All Scripture . . . is useful for giving instruction, for proof, for correcting faults, and for training in uprightness. . . ."

Inerrancy is only guaranteed when, as I have said, the thing affirmed is the author's explicit and direct concern, according to the *degree* of his affirmation, and when he proposes this truth to the assent of the reader. If he merely records an opinion —e.g. the concealment of the Ark of the Covenant as recorded in 2 Macc 2, 4ff.—the opinion may be wrong, as this one probably was, for the ark was almost certainly destroyed during the sack of Jerusalem by Nebuchadnezzar in 586; and of course he may report an erroneous statement made by someone else —e.g. Paul's statement in Acts 20, 25; since he, according to 2 Tim 4, 20, had returned to a site which he *thought* he would never see again Luke was merely faithful in recording that Paul did in fact say this.

Our concern in all these matters is to take the Bible as it is, not to make it what we would like it to be. The Bible, as we have said, is not a science manual, just as it is not history in the modern sense of "history for history's sake"—a point specifically brought out in the letter of the Biblical Commission to Cardinal Suhard which we have cited.

The Bible is a collection of divinely inspired religious books, set down by many different men, most of them Semitic thinkers, men who conceived and spoke quite differently from ourselves.

Bearing all this in mind, we reduce the strain of the doctrine of inerrancy without in any way violating its demands. The Bible is inerrant—it is "absolutely inerrant," for its writers were absolutely errorless in the work they *formally* intended to accomplish.

For those wishing further material on this important feature of biblical study, we recommend the treatise by Père Pierre Benoit, O.P., in Robert-Tricot's *Guide to the Bible*[1] or the popular booklet by Bruce Vawter, C.M., mentioned above, *The Bible is Different.*

4 THE BOOKS THAT MAKE UP THE BIBLE

IF WE CAREFULLY examine any copy of the Bible, a number of questions may easily present themselves: Why does the Bible contain these and only these books? Why is it that Jews, Protestants, and Catholics each have differing collections of books in their Bibles? How did the Bible reach its final form? Questions such as these were asked long before our times.

One thing is certain: the story of the Bible's formation is long and complicated—much more so than we customarily realize. Each book has its own formation story (how it came to be), sometimes very detailed, and there is the added story

[1] Pp. 40–52.

of how each book was received in the inspired collection technically known as the Canon of Sacred Scripture.

For all practical purposes, a book is canonical when its inspiration is officially recognized and authoritatively declared. *Canon* is a Greek word that has long served to distinguish ecclesiastical (Canon Law; canons; Canon of the Mass, etc.) from civil regulations. The use of this term in connection with Sacred Scripture goes back even further. The Greek word is probably derived from a Hebrew word *qaneh*, meaning *reed*, and then, *measure*. Gradually the concept of *norm* or *standard* became its foremost meaning. Thus when we speak of the "Canon" of Scripture, we refer to the official, *normative*, collection of inspired writings, for a book must be regarded as inspired to be placed in the Canon. In common usage, the terms "canonical" and "inspired," when applied to Scripture, designate the same meaning, for every extant inspired book is presumably in the Canon, and every canonical book is inspired.

The Old Testament Canon

The study of canonicity takes us far back into history—first Jewish, and then Christian. Involved are the factual question of the inclusion of certain books in the Jewish and Christian canons and the reasons (criteria) for placing these books there. We cannot state with certainty what standard served as a guide to Jewish religious leaders in placing certain books in their canon, while others (even referred to in the Bible, e.g. the book of Jashar, cf. Jos 10, 13) were excluded. That there was some kind of standard is generally admitted, even though the Old Testament books show an amazing diversity in theme and spirit.

The Jewish Bible (*all* of which is included in our own) grew

up around the events of the exodus from Egypt and the Mosaic
Law given in nuclear form at Sinai. What has come to be the
Pentateuch (Torah; Law; first five books of the Bible) grew
up in a most involved manner (which we hope later on to
illustrate) and was not put into *final* form until after the
Babylonian Exile (ended in 536 B.C.). All of this has been
clarified to a remarkable degree in our own time, especially
through the dual principle of ancient oral traditions and variant
written traditions, all resulting in our Pentateuch, which is the
end product of a long process. Though doubtlessly taking its
kernel and spirit from Moses, the Pentateuch is the accumulation of many strands of oral and written traditions, some of
them antedating Moses, others having arisen after his times—
but all stamped in some way with his spirit.

However, even before the Pentateuch was completed and
closed (between 500 and 400 B.C.), the next group of Old Testament books in the Hebrew Bible, the *Prophets* (including,
strangely enough, Joshua, Judges, Samuel and Kings) was near-
ing completion. This section was closed most probably during
the third century B.C.

The final section of the Hebrew Bible (which begins with
the Psalms) became known as the *Writings*. This group of books
was certainly complete by Christian times, for a special
reference is made to it (denoting it by its first book) in Lk
24, 44, and another is implicitly made in Mt 23, 35, where
the first and last books of the Hebrew Bible (Genesis and
Chronicles) are brought in. Jewish authority probably waited
until late in the first Christian century before making a final
declaration on its (now closed) Canon of Scripture.

Allowing for the fact that the Hebrew Bible contains some
ancient pre-Israelite and recast traditions, such as those regarding the first man, the early genealogies, the flood accounts, the
Old Testament was *at least* some 1,500 to 2,000 years in the
making.

From what we have said it becomes obvious that the Old Testament was only gradually formed and that to think of each book as being completed before another was begun, all in regulated order, is utterly foreign to reality. Those who wish to see this process (for the entire Old Testament) delineated in a clear and ingenious manner should consult the *Chronological Table of the Books of the Old Testament,* by Sabastiano Pagano, O.M.I.[1]

Besides those books contained in the official Jewish canon, other books gained great popularity in such important Jewish centers as Egypt. Some of these books were originally written in Greek (e.g. Wisdom and 2 Maccabees), while others were originally set down in a Semitic tongue (e.g. 1 Maccabees, Ben Sirah, Tobit). Though not forming part of an *official* canon (there was no such thing as an "Alexandrian Canon"), these books were nonetheless regarded as holy and sacred by some Jews and were accepted by the Christian Church on a par with other Old Testament books—though not without discussions and disagreements. It is this fact, precisely, that accounts for the Catholic Bible's containing seven complete books (Judith, Tobit, Ben Sirah, Wisdom, Baruch, 1 and 2 Maccabees) and parts of two others (Daniel and Esther) which are not found in either Hebrew or Protestant Bibles.

Interestingly enough, these books have turned up in some quantity at Qumrân among the famous scroll-finds and have reopened the question among non-Catholics as to their prominence and place in *Palestinian* Jewish life. A few leading Protestant scholars, e.g. Sigmund Mowinckel of Oslo, have even expressed regret that these books do not find their place in the Protestant canon: "Instead of discussing whether something is to be cut out of the Canon, or of feeling as if criticism had taken something out of it, there may be more point in

[1] This brochure can be purchased for a very small price from the University Seminary, 249 Main Street, Ottawa, Ontario, Canada.

asking whether the Protestant churches have not made a mistake in gradually cutting the ties between the so-called 'canonical' and the so-called 'apocryphal' writings of the Old Testament; for the Apocrypha belonged to Paul's Bible, the early Church's Greek Septuagint, and there are many indications that they were authoritative writings in the circles in which Jesus grew up and by which, humanly speaking, his mind was formed. The Roman Catholic Church, therefore, has maintained that the Apocrypha, too, are inspired writings. . . ."[2]

While Protestants and Jews refer to these books as *apocryphal* (i.e. of doubtful or spurious origin), we refer to them as deutero-canonical (i.e. secondarily canonical). The books which we call *apocryphal* (books included by no one today in any Bible, e.g. the recently rediscovered Gospel of Thomas), Protestants and Jews call pseudepigraphical (i.e. written under a pseudonym). Two of the finest English translations of the Bible in our times, viz. the Chicago Bible (otherwise called *An American Translation*, or the Smith-Goodspeed Bible) and the more recent *Revised Standard Version*, may both be purchased in editions that include "The Apocrypha," i.e. our deutero-canonical books. The fact that these books were included by Jews in the first and very famous translation of the Old Testament into Greek (known as the Septuagint), and that these books were not relegated to a separate section but interspersed *among* the undisputed books, is evidence enough that these books were held in high regard by pre-Christian, extra-Palestinian Jews.

While the Christian Church, with some dissenting voices, accepted the Septuagint translation (from which the New Testament draws most of its citations) and recognized its collection of books as canonical, Jews gradually abandoned this version, and never "canonized" its wider collection of books. We should

[2] *The Old Testament as the Word of God*, trans. Reidar B. Bjornard (New York, Abingdon Press, 1959), pp. 112–13.

point out, too, in all objectivity, that the Church was in no
rush to make a final, authoritative decision on the matter, for
this decision was only made definitively with the Council of
Trent (1545–1563), even though provisional and local listings
had been drawn up long before this, e.g. at Hippo in St.
Augustine's lifetime.

It was basically *apostolic tradition* that determined the
canonicity of the Old Testament books, and this operated with
considerable fluidity, especially in the early centuries of the
Church. While we find the *general* trend, both among Church
Fathers and local councils of the most disparate regions, to
accept the full canon (as it was later to be settled by Trent)
there were *for a time* noteworthy hesitations both in East and
West. But when Protestantism rejected the Old Testament deuterocanonical books (its *apocrypha*), it broke with what had
been substantially agreed upon through all Christendom for
approximately a thousand years! This was the result of Martin
Luther's having made his vernacular translation from the
Hebrew (where these books are lacking), but also it was the
result of his having rejected tradition as a valid rule of faith
(and the inclusion of these books in the Christian Bible was at
that time a matter of tradition only).

The New Testament Canon

The story of the New Testament is much less complex. Its
books were all written within a period of less than one hundred
years. Disputes centered on but seven of its books, viz. Hebrews,
James, 2 Peter, 2 and 3 John, Jude, and the Apocalypse—usually
because of some doctrinal misgivings about these books or doubtful apostolic connections. These seven books are hence termed
deuterocanonical, but have now been (re)accepted by Christians
of all faiths, even the Epistle of James finding its place now in

Lutheran Bibles, though Luther rejected it (plus Hebrews, Jude, and the Apocalypse) and dubbed it "an epistle of straw" (cf. 1 Cor 3, 12).

The New Testament books were circulated among the various churches with surprising rapidity, as is shown by 2 Pet 3, 16, where reference is made to Paul's writings, already ranked as "Scripture" and noted for their bristling and not-easily-interpreted doctrine. The earliest Church Fathers began to cite the New Testament books, though not referring to them all or stating the entire contents of the New Testament collection. The earliest citations are found in Clement of Rome (around 96 A.D.), Ignatius of Antioch (around 110), and Polycarp (around 150).

The Criteria of Canonicity

While we may be sure that some principle(s) guided Judaism in its gradual assemblage of its sacred books, we cannot be sure about the nature of the principle. Similarly, there is some vagueness that surrounds the earliest Christian criteria for accepting (a) the Old Testament books from Judaism, and (b) the New Testament books from within Christian circles. Basically, the Church must have made her decision on such grounds as: some kind of apostolic origin; liturgical use in various churches; and the type of doctrine contained in the books. It is certain that the Church never felt herself subordinate to the New Testament Scriptures, for she antedated them and it was she who would decide what was inspired and canonical. Her own sense of orthodoxy played a major role in this process of selection and rejection. On this question readers could hardly do better than take up the enjoyable and reliable little volume of Father Bruce Vawter, C.M., to which we have already referred, The Bible in the Church.

Let us not fail to mention that there was a vast body of literature (much of it still extant) roughly paralleling what we have in the canonical Scripture. This *we* call the Apocryphal writings—hundreds of them, some utterly bereft of reliability, while others are valuable witnesses to solid currents of early Christian thought. It is to the credit of the Church that she was able to slough off this inferior material and ultimately make her final decision on the books that constitute the sacred Canon of the Bible.

That the Canon of Scripture is closed for good is admitted by every Catholic scholar. Therefore we may regard as out of the question the inclusion of any other book in the Bible at some future date, even though we *may*, for the sake of discussion, admit the possibility that not all inspired books were gathered into the canonical collection.

Ultimately we rely on the decision of the Church for the precise contents of our Catholic Bible—a decision which only she, as a divinely constituted and infallible authority, can make —and it is this decision that answers the questions raised at the beginning of our discussion.

5 THE LITERAL SENSE, FOUNDATION OF SCRIPTURAL INTERPRETATION

THE MAGNIFICENT PROLOGUE to St. John's presentation of the Gospel closes with this simple-profound phrase: "No one has ever seen God. The only-begotten Son, who is in the bosom of the Father, he has revealed him" (1, 18). The Greek verb for "revealed" is *exegésato*, from which are derived our English terms *exegesis, exegete*, etc. The Greek verb means first of all "to lead out," and then "to explain or reveal." It was Christ alone who could *explain* the Father. In a dimly similar way it is the duty of the exegete to *explain the meaning* of Sacred Scripture—a duty which he will never perfectly fulfill, but which he must nonetheless keep striving to fulfill.

We must repeat once more that the Church is the ultimate and infallible interpreter of Sacred Scripture. Yet she wants the help of her scholars. Not merely does she encourage them, she commands them as her sons, as "resolute laborers in the vineyard of the Lord," to work towards clarifying the meaning of the Bible. The Church herself, to repeat the words of Pius XII, "has defined but few texts of Scripture; nor are those more numerous about which the teaching of the Holy Fathers is unanimous."

The exegete is a man from whom much is expected. Ideally, he is "thoroughly acquainted with the universal theological teaching, from which he never severs his exegetical task" (1950 *Instruction* of the Biblical Commission). By way of preparation for his work, he should be a competent linguist, both in ancient oriental and modern tongues (in which latter so many of the best biblical works are written and never translated into English!); he should be acquainted with ancient oriental history, its methods and scope; he should be familiar with the solid conclusions of Near Eastern archaeology; he should have the best possible biblical texts from which to work, etc. But his crowning work, that towards which everything else is directed, is to explain the meaning of the Bible, in whole and in part, and this task is rendered most delicate and laborious since the Bible is an entire library of the most varied types of writing; since the Bible is made up of ancient oriental literature; and since Sacred Scripture is not merely a human product, but all human and all divine. The demands placed upon the exegete in our days are such *as no other science exacts*, and this is stated in all humility, for no scholar really meets these demands to perfection.

Since Sacred Scripture is both divine and human, there have been different attitudes towards its interpretation. Some, stressing its divine aspect, have skirted whatever savors too much of the human and earthly, flying quickly to higher or apparently higher meanings. Others, stressing the human side of the Bible, have aimed at a thorough evaluation of the utterances of the human writers, not fearing to get the full impact of the human writer's meaning before attempting to scale more celestial heights. The former tendency was roughly that of the famous Alexandrian School, whose outstanding representative was Origen (died 253–254); the latter tendency was roughly that of the Antiochene School, whose truest representative was the much-calumniated Theodore of Mopsuestia (died 428). Though both schools produced their share of heresies, the Church in her recent directives has clearly opted for the Antiochene principles. These are clearly and succinctly stated in the 1943 biblical encyclical of Pius XII (*On the Most Opportune Way to Promote Biblical Studies*): "Being thoroughly prepared by the knowledge of the ancient languages and by the aids afforded by the art of criticism," he writes, "let the Catholic exegete undertake the task, of all those imposed on him the greatest, that namely of discovering and expounding the genuine meaning of the sacred books. In the performance of this task let the interpreters bear in mind that their *foremost and greatest endeavor* should be to *discern and define clearly that sense of the biblical words which is called literal*."

The literal sense is simply that meaning which the human author, divinely inspired, attaches to the words that he uses. The encyclical takes for granted the opinion now commonly held (against St. Augustine) that each passage of the Bible has *but one literal sense* (even if there may be disagreement as to what it is). If the literal sense is not one, then anything like an

objective interpretation of the Bible is made impossible. Even
if the sacred writers indulge in word-plays (cf. *wind-Spirit*
in Jn 3, 8) this very word-play is the one literal sense. Nor
is it wrong to speak of the literal sense as the *only scriptural
sense*, properly so called, for this is the meaning in the inspired
writings resulting from their dual authorship and which the
human author, with illumined judgment, intended.

Lest anyone think that we are merely interested in a stripped-
down-to-the-minimum, purely-academic, philological explanation of Scripture, we must hasten to point out that the literal
sense frequently involves the most profound theological concepts (for these were often the very intent of the sacred writer)
and that in speaking of the literal sense Pius XII goes on to
urge Catholic exegetes not to content themselves with what is
merely the groundwork leading up to the literal sense, but to
press on to its core and kernel, viz. "the theological doctrine
in faith and morals of the individual books or texts." It was
precisely because some Catholic scholars were negligent in this
regard that "some took refuge in a certain spiritual and, as
they say, mystical interpretation" (Pius XII). This "mystical
interpretation," which doubtlessly alludes to the Indexed work
of Dolindo Ruotolo (spoken of above), is one not founded on
the solid basis of the literal sense; in other words, it is not a
genuine meaning of the Bible. It is a meaning injected into
Sacred Scripture. It is accommodation—a process from which
Pius XII tells us to "scrupulously refrain."

Every recent Roman biblical document has emphasized the
literal sense. Benedict XV in his 1920 encyclical cites St. Jerome
as asserting that "in the first place we must study the literal
or historical meaning . . . all interpretation rests on the literal
sense." The 1941 *Letter* of the Biblical Commission mentions
"the grave exaggeration of the Alexandrian School, wishing to
find a symbolical meaning everywhere, even to the detriment
of the literal and historical meaning of the text." It quotes St.

Thomas as saying: "All the senses are founded on one—the literal—from which alone can any argument be drawn." It counsels that "before everything else, one must seek out the literal sense." The 1950 *Instruction* of the same Commission and the 1950 encyclical *On Various Theological and Philosophical Errors (Humani Generis)* repeat the same principles, condemning a spurious "symbolical or spiritual exegesis."

It is interesting that so spiritual a thinker and writer (though he will never go down in history as a really great exegete) as St. Bonaventure states: "The man who spurns the letter of Sacred Scripture will never rise to its spiritual meanings."

All that we have said amounts to this: in interpreting Sacred Scripture we must build on a firm foundation, and that foundation is only established by getting at the very roots of the author's intended meaning. Let us repeat once more: this meaning is not infrequently *loaded* with the most profound (or lofty) theological thought.

The story, however, is not yet complete. Pius XII goes on to speak of a valid "spiritual sense." "For what was said and done in the Old Testament was ordained and disposed by God with such consummate wisdom that things past prefigured in a spiritual way those that were to come under the dispensation of grace. Wherefore the exegete, just as he must search out and expound the literal meaning of the words, intended and expressed by the sacred writer, *so also must he do likewise for the spiritual sense*, provided it is clearly intended by God. For God alone could have known this spiritual meaning and have revealed it to us."

What the pontiff refers to as "spiritual sense" is at times called "typology," whereby persons, things, or events in the Old Testament serve as "types"—divinely intended prefigurement of New Testament or eternal realities. Thus David typifies Christ, the hoped-for king; the manna typifies the Holy Eucharist; the Egyptian exodus typifies the redemptive work of

Christ who leads us out of bondage and darkness to freedom and light. This "spiritual sense" might also include the controverted "fuller sense," a more profound understanding of Old Testament thought in the light of further revelation—though good scholars have seen fit to place it in the category of literal sense (e.g. Pierre Benoit, O.P.), specifying that it was *not perceived* by the inspired writer of a text in question, e.g. Mary, in Gen 3, 15.

It would be hard to ask for more solid directives than those of Pius XII. His encyclical is a masterpiece of precision and wisdom, offering at once the most solid scientific principles and the loftiest spiritual ideals. Readers could hardly do better than to acquire a copy of this encyclical and read it through with absolute thoroughness.

It is ironical that we have some accommodations of the Old Testament in the New (a process that was not frowned upon in a less scientific age; cf. e.g. what is said of Melkizedek in Hebrews 7, 3), among the Church Fathers, in the sacred liturgy, and in the sermons of some great masters of sacred eloquence. There is no doubt of this fact. Yet Pius XII states that accommodation "should be used with moderation and restraint" and that, "especially in these days, it is not free from danger, since the faithful, in particular those who are well-informed in the sciences sacred and profane, wish to know what God has told us in the Sacred Letters rather than what an ingenious orator or writer may suggest by a clever use of the words of Scripture." Not only is this practice "extrinsic and accidental" to Scripture, but the Word of God "does not need artificial devices and human adaptations to move and impress people. Its pages are "of themselves rich in original meaning, endowed with a divine power. . . ."

The question of the "senses of Sacred Scripture" is complicated, nor do all Catholic scholars agree on secondary issues. The basic principles, however, are settled and clear. It is the literal sense, whether it comes to us as metaphor, parable, poetry, or prose—or in any other way—that stands as the firm foundation of the whole edifice of biblical doctrine. Readers desirous of more exhaustive information on this topic could not find better material than that presented in Robert-Tricot's *Guide to the Bible*,[1] in the section on *Interpretation*, and in the references given in the index under *Senses of Sacred Scripture*.

6   *WHICH VERSION OF THE BIBLE SHOULD YOU READ?*

CATHOLICS are in no way obligated by law to read the Bible. In fact, during a time of stress, two Roman pontiffs (Paul IV in 1559 and Sixtus V in 1590) decreed that permission from the Holy Office was required before reading the Bible in vernacular translation! Happily such a state of affairs did not long endure.

Throughout the long history of the Church it has been the *privilege* of Catholics to read the Bible, and the strongest encouragement and exhortation in this regard has often been given to her children by the Church. St. Jerome, addressed in the liturgy as "the greatest teacher in interpreting Sacred Scripture," went so far as to say that "ignorance of Scripture is ignorance of Christ." Yet the Church does not force us—she merely invites us "to drink deep of both Old and New Testaments, for in both we find Christ" (St. Ambrose).

Catholics of our time are faced with a very practical problem with regard to the Bible, and that is which version of the

[1] Pp. 678–780.

Bible they should use. Note that we have used the word "version"—for this means *translation*. When we speak of "text" of the Bible we refer to the original texts (none of which have been preserved for us in their absolutely original copies ["autographs"]). Texts are in Hebrew (most of the Old Testament), Aramaic (e.g. parts of Daniel and Ezra), or Greek (some of the Old Testament and all of the New Testament). Since few are in a position to work with these texts, most Bible readers must rely on a version if they they are to receive "the encouragement of the Scriptures" (Rom 15, 4).

It will not hurt to state once more that it is the original texts that were primarily inspired. Versions are inspired *equivalently*, i.e. insofar as they faithfully transmit the thought and spirit of the original text. It is of the greatest importance, then, to have the best translation possible, for not all of them are marked by the same excellence.

The Bible has been translated into many languages, often (as in English) many times over. The very first version of the Bible was the Septuagint (Greek) translation of the Old Testament. This version was made only gradually (roughly from 250 to 150 B.C.), and shows the marks of different workmen of unequal talent. Other Greek and various Latin versions were made in the early Christian era before the time of St. Jerome.

In the Christian West the Latin Vulgate translation, largely the work of St. Jerome, gradually gained the ascendancy and, despite vernacular translations, really reigned supreme until 1943. It was then that Pius XII re-explained the position of the Vulgate and urged translations from the original texts (which he termed "better than any, even the best translations")—no longer from the Vulgate. Hence the post-1943 trend.

As far as *complete* English translations of the Bible are concerned, Catholics have at their disposal the Douay-Rheims version (in its various revised forms), now regarded as obsolete and in line for respectful but undelayed retirement. They also have the complete Bible as translated *from the Vulgate* (with an eye to the original texts) by the great British scholar, Msgr. Ronald Knox. This version has distinct merits, especially along literary lines, and has won not a few Catholics over to Bible reading. Knox at times offers very precious insights into the meaning of biblical passages.[1]

The Catholic Biblical Association of America under sponsorship of the Confraternity of Christian Doctrine is producing a complete version of the Bible. The New Testament (from the Vulgate) came out in 1941. Next (in 1952) came Volume I of the Old Testament (including the first eight books, and translated from the Hebrew). In 1955 came Volume III of the Old Testament (containing the seven Wisdom books). Volume IV made its appearance in early 1961, and Volume II is about a year away from being ready for publication. Furthermore, while the work on the Old Testament is good, it is not what it might be, *especially as regards footnotes.* The New Testament is being completely retranslated from the original Greek text. It is impossible to say when the complete Confraternity Bible will appear, and it is going to be a work of unequal value unless an over-all revision is made. Furthermore, it is too expensive to buy five separate volumes—four of which are now on the market and one of which will be replaced (the New Testament). While Germany, France, Spain, and Italy have several Catholic versions—all from the original texts—we do not as yet have one!

There is every reason to hope that a *substantial* English edition of the famous Jerusalem Bible (in French) will be given us by Father Alexander Jones of Upholland, England. This was promised for 1958 at one time, but obstacles have arisen that may put its completion somewhat beyond 1962. This, we may reasonably expect, will be a valuable addition to our English

[1] Cf. R. A. Dyson, S.J., in *Catholic Biblical Quarterly,* 19 (October 1957), pp. 488–89, for more detailed observations on this version.

Bibles; for the Jerusalem Bible is one of the best translation-presentations of the Bible that have been made. It is equipped with introductions, reliable footnotes, divisional headings, and valuable cross-references.

We are, of course, blessed with a number of good English translations of the New Testament by Catholics, e.g. Westminster, Spencer, and Kleist-Lilly—all of them from the original texts. These may all be recommended, especially for their accuracy, if not for their English excellence.

But our problem is a *complete Bible* in good, accurate, and readable translation, and what we are about to consider will probably appear as a drastic solution to many of our readers. Nonetheless, it is backed by responsible Church authorities.

There are several English translations of the entire Bible by non-Catholics (groups or individuals)—translations that are recognized by all (including Catholics) as objectively reliable and accurate. We refer especially to the Smith-Goodspeed Bible (popularly known as the *Chicago Bible*, or *An American Translation*); the *Revised Standard Version;* or that by James Moffatt. The first two translations may be purchased in editions that include our deuterocanonical books, even though they are set aside in a special section called *The Apocrypha.* Catholics who consider themselves *in any way* students of Sacred Scripture may make use of these versions, for none of them contain doctrinal footnotes.[2] This view is backed by theologians of the highest repute as well as by the concrete fact that the Catholic Bishop of Copenhagen, Denmark, has adopted a non-Catholic version of the Bible for Catholic use in the whole of Denmark, *even though Catholic versions exist.* To this non-Catholic version have been added the footnotes and introduction (in Danish translation) of the Jerusalem Bible. In more than half of our own American seminaries, the Chicago Bible is used in class in preference to Catholic versions of the Scriptures.

[2] Cf. *Worship* (July–August, 1958), pp. 416–19.

There are, of course, instances in these non-Catholic translations where the rendering will strike us as weak, e.g. Phil 4, 4 in the Chicago Bible: "Goodbye, and the Lord be with you always. Again I say, goodbye."[3] But the really doctrinal texts are frequently translated with a commendable thoroughness, e.g. Mt. 16, 18 in the Chicago Bible: "But I tell you, your name is Peter, a rock, and on this rock I will build my church and the powers of death shall not subdue it."[4]

We may offer, therefore, as at least a temporary solution to our biblical needs, the suggestion that Catholics use the above-mentioned versions of the Bible.

It is also of interest that work has now been begun on a common, inter-faith Bible. Not only is a Catholic priest on the editorial board of this Bible (to come out in many separate inexpensive volumes), but at least two books (that we know of) are being done by Catholic priest-scholars, viz. Mitchell Dahood, S.J., an American teaching at the Roman Pontifical Biblical Institute, who is doing the Psalms; and Raymond Brown, S.S., of Baltimore.

In our days—and for this we may be grateful—biblical studies are being carried on by scholars of all faiths in a remarkable spirit of objectivity. Biased translations are less and less common (though the Jehovah's Witness version, "The World Translation," is notably tendentious). It is for this reason that we need not have the fears with regard to non-Catholic translations that were once so common.

It is doubtful that we will ever reach a final translation of the Bible. The reason for this is simple. There is so much new light coming in on the meaning of Hebrew, Aramaic, and Greek terms, not to speak of the other related oriental languages, that we will always be in a position to improve our translations. It

[3] J. M. Powis Smith and Edgar J. Goodspeed, eds., *Complete Bible, An American Translation* (Chicago, University of Chicago Press, 1935).
[4] *Ibid.*

is for this reason that many scholars are not really interested in a definitive version of the Bible. They do not want scholarship frozen at any one point. This should not alarm us, for our best translations today will never be far from reliable. The Jerusalem Bible in but ten years has already begun its third, revised edition—yet the changes are not astounding. They are mostly of a minor character.

Translations differ in their spirit and purpose, too. Some translators aim at the idiom of common parlance; others try to be slavishly literal; still others strive for a reverential tone. All of these translations have their purpose; yet they must convey the *meaning* of the original text if they are to be regarded as good translations.

The Church will always be solicitous about the translation of the Bible that her children use. This is not merely her right. It is her duty. Conditions today have made it possible for her to grant liberties that she could not reasonably have granted in earlier times and under different conditions.

We may only hope that Catholics today will take advantage of their opportunities and once again familiarize themselves with the inspired Word of God. This is not only to their personal advantage. It is to the advantage of the entire Church, and to the ecumenical movement in which the Bible must, of necessity, play a large part. The Bible, situated in the genuine setting of tradition, is, as much as anything else, bringing the Christian denominations together. Catholics, as Jaroslav Pelikan (author of *The Riddle of Roman Catholicism*) has stated, are re-examining their Bibles; Protestants are re-examining tradition.

7 *ISRAELITE PRE-HISTORY: GENESIS 1—11*

THE EXPLANATION of the first eleven chapters of Genesis has never proved to be an easy task. St. Augustine made three major attempts at it but always found his work dissatisfying. Nonetheless, these chapters are among the most important in the entire Bible, dealing as they do with cosmic and human origins and with some of the most delicate and vital questions that concern mankind. Our purpose in this chapter is to set the stage for the later consideration of particular questions connected with this section of the Bible.

It is my conviction that we are in a better position today than ever before in the history of Christian exegesis to evaluate these chapters correctly. This does not mean that the task has become easy; it does mean that we have better and surer tools to work with, and sounder principles to guide us than our predecessors had. Let us also hope that we can profit from the mistakes that others have made.

The present chapter has two specific objectives: first, to see these first eleven chapters of Genesis in relationship to the rest of the Pentateuch (otherwise called the Torah; the Law; or the first five books of the Bible); second, to discuss the *literary form* of these chapters. By this we mean the intent and methods of the writers; the objectivity and historicity of these chapters; the particular aspect(s) under which these chapters are offered to us by the inspired authors.

*Genesis 1—11 in the General Context
of the Pentateuch*

In an earlier chapter we pointed out that the Pentateuch was the first section of the Old Testament to reach its final form. This took place somewhere between 500 and 400 B.C. However, a long history led up to this final shaping of the Pentateuch, and we must beg the reader's patience and indulgence as we attempt to take him through what is admittedly a complicated, difficult, and sometimes dry process.

It is customary both in Judaism and Christianity to speak of Moses as the author of the Pentateuch, and the Bible itself has something to say on the subject. Just check Lk 16, 29; 24, 27; and Jn 1, 17 as samples. Today, after the question of Mosaic authorship has passed through something of a crisis, the most critical scholars are quite willing to admit that the Pentateuch is *substantially* the work of the great Hebrew lawgiver; that it everywhere bears the stamp of his spirit; and that Moses is something like a filter or prism through which all the material in the Pentateuch has somehow passed, reflecting his spirit, even if there is not absolute harmony or agreement in the resulting product.

To speak more concretely, a good share of the material in the Pentateuch existed in *oral* (the orientals have always had tenacious and phenomenal memories) *or written* form long before the time of Moses (who died around 1250 B.C.). If these materials were not actually handled by Moses, they were dealt with by later compilers in accord with his spirit. This is true of the very chapters of Genesis that we propose to discuss.

Moses himself *without any doubt* set down at least the kernel of the Pentateuch in writing (especially the Ten Commandments, and some of the positive—as distinguished from the casuistic—law). He may have passed on other information

orally—a factor that is being taken into ever greater consideration, thanks to the research of Scandinavian scholars.

However, after the death of Moses, *variant* traditions, at first
oral and then written, began to arise at the different sanctuaries
where the Hebrew people were instructed by priests and
prophets. This was especially true after the North-South split
under Rehoboam in 931 B.C. (cf. 1 Sm 12, 1–19).

As a result of this we are now accustomed to speak of these
variant traditions in a language that at first glance seems destined
only for scholars but which is really not so difficult as it looks.
The oldest identifiable tradition is termed J (coming from the
German "Jahwe," which corresponds to our Yahweh, the most
characteristic Hebrew name for God). J reached a state of
crystallization somewhere in the ninth century B.C. in the
southern kingdom of Judah, and is represented, e.g., in Gen 2,
4b up to Gen 5, 1. This tradition is noted for its early use of
the name "Yahweh" for God (though another tradition states
that this name was only revealed to Moses), but *much more*
for its very concrete way of expressing things, often describing
God in a human manner—e.g. God walks, works in clay, makes
garments, repents, is pleased with the sweet odor of sacrifice,
asks questions, plants a garden. The J tradition has a marvellous
way of putting across great theological ideas through the use of
the simplest imagery and symbolism.

Another tradition, called E (since it uses the name "Elohim"
for God), took shape at a slightly later date in the northern
kingdom of Israel. It is not so widely represented in the Pentateuch, but nonetheless sets forth its own account of events or
laws, being noted for its moral refinement. It is *not represented
at all* in the first eleven chapters of Genesis.

Very important is the P (Priestly) tradition. This took final
shape *after* the Babylonian exile (therefore after 536 B.C.) and
is noted for its refined theological expression, usually avoiding
the vigorous human language that J cherishes. The P tradition

has the honor of being represented at the very beginning of the Bible, from Gen 1, 1 up to Gen 2, 4a, where it provides us with the famous six-day creation story.

The D tradition (found mostly in the book of Deuteronomy) took form between 750 and 650 B.C. and therefore antedates P. But as it doesn't concern us too much at the present, it is here placed last. As far as Gen 1—11 is concerned, *only* J and P are involved.

This might seem like so much pedantry—but it isn't. *The first eleven chapters of Genesis* (and many other parts of the Bible) *cannot be truly understood without a recognition of these traditions.* It is the presence of variant traditions that accounts for two or more variant stories of the same event; it explains the all too obvious jarring of ideas that we at times find in the Bible; it illustrates most clearly the very different concept of history writing and narrative used by the ancient orientals.

There is something remarkably similar in our four Gospels. There is actually but *one Gospel,* that of Christ, first delivered orally, by the way. The canonical Scriptures give *four presentations* of that Gospel, *according to* Mark, Matthew, Luke, and John (and there is a reason for placing Mark first—since, *as we have them now,* Mark is the most primitive presentation of the four). Modern historiographers could hardly follow the methodology used in the Bible, where variant traditions are allowed to speak for themselves with scant effort made at harmonization and minute agreement. The biblical writers obviously worked differently from modern historians and made no pretense of following the canons that govern present-day critical methods. The evidence for this in the Bible is overwhelming, as careful readers soon note for themselves.

Our present Pentateuch, then, is not the work of a Moses who sat down and penned out five books in succession—as was held by some Catholic scholars not too many years ago! The Pentateuch is a collection, even an accumulation, of incidents, anecdotes, popular accounts, laws, etc., that grew up over a long period of time and was set in final form by an editor or group of editors between 500 and 400 B.C.

The Pentateuch is based primarily, though not exclusively, on the four major traditions that we outlined above. The Pentateuch is a compilation, its kernel being the events connected with the *exodus* from Egypt, the law bestowal, and covenant rites at Mt. Sinai. *All later legislation*, whether in strict accord or not, was fitted into the framework of the life of Moses, even though in some cases it was made hundreds of years after his death and bore evident signs of modification.

Too, the historical interests of the Hebrew people gradually led them to investigate their past, going back *before* the time of the exodus. This brought about the compilation of the *patriarchal family history* that we find in Gen 12—50. Finally, they wished to go back even earlier than their patriarchs, beyond their father, Abraham, and this led to the compilation of materials that we find in Gen 1—11. Only J and P seem to have worked out this earlier history, just as Matthew and Luke are the only Evangelists to give us an Infancy Narrative, which was not a part of the primitive Gospel catechesis.

All of this stands up quite solidly once we realize what a tremendous event the exodus (with the Sinai incidents) was for the Hebrew people. The prophets would not allow the people to forget that it was through the exodus that God intervened on their behalf as never before, and that in entering into a covenant with him at Sinai they had been favored as no other people had been.

All this must be said (and should even be said in greater detail) if we are to realize that the first eleven chapters of Genesis are a section of Scripture that stands off by itself. This is true since the material in these eleven chapters takes us back before the time of Abraham. Hence the material in these eleven chapters was originally *not Hebrew property*, nor could it have been. The material was largely taken over from the stories of other peoples, but was *carefully recast* in the light of Hebrew theology and monotheism. We say this with strong conviction for the simple reason that if the material had been directly revealed to the sacred writers (or to Moses), we would not find it presented in *variant* manners, and this it obviously is in many aspects.

Modern biblical scholars are agreed that not only did the Hebrew writers make their "research" on cosmic and human origins rather late in their history, but also that much of the material set forth in these chapters is comparable to accounts current among other nations. The discovery of other flood stories, of other creation accounts, of other sin accounts, *all within the last hundred years,* has opened up an entire new vista on these eleven chapters.

Yet, and this is most important, though the Bible has undeniable similarities to the other accounts, its presentation is remarkable for its purity of expression and loftiness of theology —thus differentiating itself in a distinct manner from the pagan accounts. Gen 1—11, let us emphatically state, is not entirely paralleled in the non-biblical accounts, nor will it probably ever be.

This fact, and the superiority of the biblical narratives, makes us ask where the biblical writers—in this case J and P, plus the final editor(s)—got their information. Was it through revelation? It need not have been, and the variant accounts within these eleven chapters render this less and less probable. Was it through an enlightened borrowing of material from the other nations? This seems to be *partly* the case, but cannot answer for everything in Gen 1—11. Very likely the writers, under divine inspiration to be sure, indulged in what we can only call some "reconstruction work." This is even more likely now that the great antiquity of rational man on this earth is so firmly established.

This much is certain. The biblical writers have not given us a scientific account, and therefore we must not fall into the trap of *concordism*, spoken of earlier. The whole emphasis is on religion, on theological lessons, on the plan of salvation. To repeat, if there is anything that we have learned (by sad and painful experience) it is that the Bible is not a science manual.

Gen 1—11, then, took its rise through a rather involved process—materials being borrowed, "reconstructed," recast, and then incorporated into the two major traditions that we call J and P. Finally, editors combined these materials as they deemed best, thus giving us Gen 1—11.

The Literary Form of Genesis 1—11

When Cardinal Suhard wrote to the Biblical Commission the letter to which we have referred above, asking if the Commission could tell him how "historical" were the first eleven chapters of Genesis, his was a gesture of the greatest filial loyalty. The Commission's answer was of necessity somewhat vague, speaking of the obscurity and complexity of the question and putting the burden of its solution on biblical scholars, who must study "all of the literary, scientific, historical, cultural and religious problems connected with these chapters." Even the *"very notion of historical truth* among the early orientals" was recommended for closer study. The Commission stated that these eleven chapters are not historical in our modern sense of the word, but it warned that we must not therefore jump to the conclusion that they are bereft of history and hence unhistorical. In recent times (June 20, 1961) the Holy Office has admonished biblical scholars to deal most carefully with the matter of history in the Bible.

Perhaps we might term these chapters "popular religious

history." Not a few Catholic scholars have even used the term "folklore" with regard to *some* incidents in these eleven chapters (e.g. the Babel story). For the moment we must leave this question somewhat "in the air." Actually, there are different literary forms within these eleven chapters, and we can only classify them as we take up particular incidents.

Those readers who wish to delve more deeply into the generalities of these first eleven chapters may refer to the *Guide to the Bible*,[1] and to the many references given there. We also invite you to read these first eleven chapters attentively, but also reverently, looking for the lessons that this section of the Bible intends to convey to its readers.

8 *THE SIX-DAY CREATION ACCOUNT: GENESIS 1, 1–2, 4a*

GENESIS, as we have seen, is compiled from a number of traditions that reach far back into, and even partially beyond, Israel's own history. Before they were ever set down in writing, these traditions were passed on, from generation to generation, in *oral* form. Yet, as ancient as they are, they could hardly go back as far as the appearance of rational man on earth.

The first creation account in Genesis, from 1, 1 to 2, 4a (it stops right in the middle of the verse!), is to be read as a unit. It derives from the Priestly tradition, having reached its final form, as we saw, somewhere around 500 B.C. The account is stamped with a genuinely priestly spirit (interest in cult) and

[1] Robert-Tricot, *op. cit.*, pp. 171–76.

is thoroughly constructed, showing signs of long and careful planning. Its symmetrical form would have considerably facilitated its being committed to memory.

Though this account is washed clean of the mythology and polytheism, the curious "births" and struggles, that characterize other ancient oriental creation stories (such as the *Enuma Elish* story from ancient Mesopotamia, written on seven tablets), there *are* some points of contact between these stories and Genesis—yet always to the credit of the biblical write-up. The doctrinal purity and uncompromising monotheism of our account are truly amazing, especially when we consider the smallness of Israel as against the size of the nations whose muddled stories she so far surpassed or completely rejected.

The Priestly account conveys a number of very important theological ideas. It is precisely these that we should look for and attempt to penetrate, since they were foremost in the mind of the writer(s). When we say "theological," we must be satisfied with a theology less refined and formal than our own, yet reducible to our theological conceptions.

The great and primary lesson in this account is God's unique position as Creator of everything that exists. With majestic effortlessness and complete transcendency he has produced every creature. Sun, moon, and stars, so often the object of worship in the ancient Near East, are his *creatures.* The sun and moon are even referred to by the somewhat degrading names of "large and small luminaries" since their Semitic names (Shemesh and Yareah) suggest false deities. Note both the positive teaching and the clever polemics in this account.

God's creative act, we may add, is not viewed as belonging to the *merely* scientific or cosmic realm. It is rather viewed by the Priestly writer as the *first* in a never-ending series of "salvation acts"—the wonderful interventions of God in our life as he leads us to ultimate salvation. We need not maintain that the Priestly school had arrived at the full concept of "creation from nothing," for this involves philosophic speculation foreign to the ancient Hebrew mentality. Yet, neither should we excessively debilitate their notion of creation. It is God who had both produced and ordered the universe. A fuller notion of "creation" will be formulated by the devout Jewish mother in 2 Macc 7, 28.

The Priestly writer had another major concern in mind as he drew up the creation account before us. This, as we have already noted, was Sabbath observance, something characteristic of Judaism (and, we might add, of us). In order to put this observance across in a forceful manner, and perhaps at the same time to combat the seven-tablet Babylonian creation story, he chose to fit all the major creation works into a six-day period, an *artificial* framework to be sure, comparable to *six regular working days.* When these days were complete and God's creation work was finished, he would "rest," i.e. cease from his task, thus offering an example to faithful Jews and showing that the Sabbath is a divinely sanctioned institution. There is a remarkable similarity of language here and in Exod 20, 8ff. (where the Sabbath is treated)—so similar that it leaves no doubt of the link-up between the two accounts, both of them coming from the Priestly tradition. We must insist that the six-day creation scheme is an artificial device, even though it employs twenty-four-hour days (otherwise the Sabbath lesson would be considerably weakened). We need not believe that God actually created everything in six days. That is a scientific question—not the concern of the biblical writer. Very few scholars today, as we have already pointed out, would be ensnared by any such interpretation as six days of "thousands of years" each, etc., based as it is on an unreliable "concordism" (implying that the Bible teaches "science" as much as religion) and on an equally unreliable geology. The fact that the Biblical Commission *allowed* such an interpretation ("certain space of time") in 1909 was what one great scholar termed "the last respects paid to a dying concordism."

The evening and morning are signs of a normal (Jewish) day, beginning with sunset (even today the Jewish Sabbath begins Friday evening—welcoming in the Sabbath—and closes Saturday evening).

A third aim of the writer, as already hinted at, was to combat false worship, whether with regard to the Babylonian deities (some Jews had but recently returned from the Babylonian Captivity when this account was written), or the widespread Near Eastern cult of sun, moon, stars, and other creatures.

The writer, furthermore, wished to bring out the *excellence* of man over all other visible creatures. Hence man is created last (though we are not told in this account *how* this takes place, as the Yahwist (J) writer will do in Gen 2, 7ff.), for the writer ascends from lower to higher creatures. Though our writer hardly touches on the question of man and woman (of such great interest to the J writer), he does wish to tell us of man's lofty dignity: he is made "to the image and likeness of God." This means, as the context shows, that man shares in God's *dominion* over creatures lower than himself. It *implies* that man has higher faculties enabling him to exercise this dominion intelligently and wisely—but the ancient Hebrew did not speak of "higher faculties," such as intellect and will.

Still a fifth aim of the Priestly writer was to stress the utter *goodness* of all that God made. As each work is completed, its goodness is emphasized. If the Priestly writer ever went into the question of the origin of evil and of man's fall from divine friendship we have no record of it, for what Genesis gives us on that question is taken entirely from the J writer. When the Priestly narrative ends with 2, 4a, we can turn to 5, 1 and note that the story is carried right on, for that is where the Priestly writer's account is resumed.

There are doubtless other lessons of a minor nature in this

creation story, but we have listed those that stand out more clearly. As long as we stress what the writer stressed, the account loses none of its value for us today.

It is quite likely (and this is no isolated instance) that the story as we now have it was worked over from a more primitive form. Thus we note that the third and sixth day are each "overloaded," including two works in place of one. This does not unduly mar the symmetry of the six days, however, and it has long been pointed out how the first day (light) corresponds to the fourth (the heavenly luminaries: sun, moon, stars, as distributors of the light); the second day (water is divided by the firmament) corresponds to the fifth (water and air creatures); and that the third day (separation of dry land *and* plant life) corresponds to the sixth (living creatures upon the earth *and* man). This is not a "scientific" ordering of creation. It is largely "mnemonic," i.e. helpful to memorization, and is based upon ancient oriental ideas common to other peoples besides the Hebrews. Thus we have light before the sun (for the sun was regarded not so much as a light-giver as a place where light gathers); we have the stress upon primeval water and darkness—signs of chaos and disorder. We shall recall from an earlier chapter that the idea of the firmament, a solid, inverted, bowl-like covering, high-up over the earth, holding aloft vast stores of water—that could be released by opening the "gates of heaven" (cf. Gen 7, 11)—was common in the ancient orient. The earth, too, was regarded as saucer-shaped, floating on water and held up by pillars that sank way down in the abyss below. These and other indications should make us realize that this is not a "scientific" account. Nor is it entirely correct to describe the narrative as "popular," as least *if* we imply that the writer could have written scientifically had he wished to do so. God does not ordinarily infuse such advanced knowledge into the minds of his inspired instruments—especially when it has little to do with the primary purpose of the Sacred Writings. St. Thomas laid down the sound principle that the "sacred writers went by what sensibly appeared" (*Summa Theologica,* 1a, q. 70, a.1, ad 3).

The Priestly writer has produced a marvellous document, quite sufficient for his purposes. Readers who want to see how superior the biblical story is should get a copy of *Ancient Near East: An Anthology of Texts and Pictures,* edited by James B. Pritchard,[1] and read some of the other creation stories. They will note the points in common, but also the gulf that separates the biblical account from those of the other nations.

Let us now have a look at some special points of this creation account. It is of interest that St. John opens his Gospel presentation with words borrowed from Gen 1, 1. John says: "In the beginning was the Word" (he is referring to the second Person of the Blessed Trinity). Genesis says: "In the beginning God created heaven and earth"—a summary statement of the entire creation story, for the Hebrews had no exact word for "universe" and had to paraphrase by saying "heaven(s) and earth." In both cases the idea of *pre-existence* is present—in Genesis, God existed before visible (and invisible) creation; in John, the Word existed before all things were made. It is in this manner that John teaches the full divinity of Christ.

What about the "spirit of God" hovering over the chaotic watery mass in Gen 1, 2? Is this the Holy Spirit, third person of the Blessed Trinity? Though so applied by some ecclesiastical writers and liturgical texts, it is hard to accept this as the literal sense of the passage. This "spirit of God" would best be translated as a "mighty wind," for the Hebrews frequently used the term "God" as an adjective in order to bring out greatness, e.g. Ps 68, 16, and 104, 16. It is doubtful that the "mighty wind" has anything to do with creative work at all. It merely adds to the general description of chaotic primitive creation before the work of adornment begins.

Many Christian writers have likewise been tempted to see a

[1] Princeton, Princeton University Press, 1958.

Trinitarian reference in Gen 1, 26: "Let *us* make man to *our* image and likeness . . ." the plural usage being seen as a veiled hint at plurality of persons in God. Of course, once the Trinity is revealed to us in the New Testament we rightly assume that God was a Trinity at the moment of creation—but that does not mean that this text, as set down by the inspired writer, refers to the Blessed Trinity. It more likely refers to the richness of God, whose name is often pluralized in the Bible (Elohim is plural). The Hebrews frequently pluralized rich concepts such as "life" and "blood."

The creation account in Genesis loses nothing of its everlasting importance and meaning when understood in its genuine literal meaning. Its impact may strike the reader of the twentieth century as forcibly as the reader of the sixth-fifth centuries B.C. With the benefit of the intervening Christian revelation and our recovery of much of the oriental background, we may even profit more from the account today than the readers of old.

Speaking before the Pontifical Academy of Sciences on November 22, 1951, Pope Pius XII referred to the material universe as being between five and ten billion years old! He added: "Although these figures may seem astounding, even to the simplest faithful they bring no new or different concept from the one they learned in the opening words of the book of Genesis."

9 THE YAHWIST STORY OF THE GARDEN IN EDEN: GENESIS 2, 4b–25

THE PRIESTLY STORY of creation breaks off abruptly in the very center of Gen 2, 4 as the general editor of Genesis introduces the Yahwist (J) tradition. Superficially, this tradition takes its name from the fact that it uses Yahweh as the name for God. However, its differences from the Priestly tradition (P) are much more profound than this, entailing a distinct outlook and manner of presentation. The J tradition (we will often refer to this as the J writer, or simply J) which, as we saw, arose around the ninth century B.C., is noted for its imagery, symbolism, human ways of speaking about God (anthropomorphisms), chattiness, and a certain lack of theological refinement. Behind all this, however, lie the most vital lessons and realities. J is interested in theological *significance* rather than in historical niceties; and yet he would not have us look upon his writing as bereft of historical reliability—far from it! Here, as much as anywhere in the Bible, we feel the real difficulty of classifying the literary form. At the same time this is of paramount importance if we are to grasp the full impact of J's narrative. The Church's directives have never chosen to say the last word on this question, leaving scholars considerable liberty in her decrees ranging all the way from 1909 up 1948.

Although this section of Genesis (2, 4b–25) is sometimes called the "second creation account," this is not the best way to describe it. J does not have the same cosmic interests as the P writer and is not so much interested in the creation of the world as he is in *man*. J has his own preoccupations, methods, and, we might add, *genius*. J is a subtle and accomplished theologian, yet always in the Hebrew sense, which is a far cry from the formal language of scholasticism. J, to put it briefly, wants to convey the loftiest and weightiest theological notions through the simplest of images and symbols. We can only do him justice by attempting to catch his lessons.

We might add that J set out to answer a number of very intriguing and vital questions, such as: How did man (and woman) originate? What is their relationship to one another and to God? How did sin and evil find their way into human life? Why do men and women suffer, each after his or her own special manner? What hope does the future offer? The heavily symbolic and imaged stories that J is going to relate all the way from Gen 2, 4b up as far as 5, 1 (where P takes over again) were meant to answer these questions. And, let us not forget, J answers these questions as an inspired writer, and hence as an errorless writer in the sense in which *he intended* his account.

Let us once more posit a question which we can only partially answer, Where did J get his information? There is absolutely no doubt that he was acquainted with some of the stories, legends, and myths that were in circulation at his time. These he utilized to some limited degree, yet always recasting them, correcting them, and more often rejecting them as he set forth his own superior account. J, too, must have done no small amount of *reconstruction work*, judging the past by the present, analyzing most keenly the constant traits of human nature, and taking care to write in a manner that is more of a theological instruction than a "tape-recording" of the events of early man. We are forced to these conclusions by what we now know of the ancient past and especially by what we know of man's long life on earth. Few scholars today allow that the stories related by J could have been handed down over thousands of years (perhaps 200,000 years or more!) in any kind of accurate form. J *may* have received some kind of revelation, yet this *need not* be the case. He assuredly had a marvellous sense of "orthodoxy," and of course did his work (though he need not have known about it) under divine inspiration and guidance.

Let us now take up chapter 2 of Genesis, going from verse 4b to 25 (the end of the chapter), limiting ourselves to the more essential remarks. Much more can be and is said than we are able to say in this chapter. More ambitious readers are invited to study the volume by Hauret entitled *Beginnings: Genesis and Modern Science* to which we have already referred, or the equally excellent work by Bruce Vawter, C.M., *A Path Through Genesis.*[1] What we are going to discuss here *sets the stage* for the extremely important material of chapter 3 (which we will take up next).

Unlike the P account, our narrative assumes a "dry" state of affairs in the beginning. It is only with verse 6, however obscure it may be, that water is introduced into the story. Likewise, there is only one day in the J narrative—not six of them. Obviously, the general editor of Genesis felt no need to "harmonize" the P and J traditions. J's order of creation (man, then animals and birds, and finally woman) stands in marked contrast to that of P in chapter one.

Hurrying past the "cosmic" part of his account, J quickly rivets his attention on Man. Man is God's creature, having both an earthy and sublime side. Not knowing much about the actual first man, J avoids details; he generalizes and reconstructs. He presents God as a divine Potter, forming Man from the clay of the earth. (There is an obvious Hebrew word-play between *adam* [Man] and *adamah* [earth] in the original text.) When Man (to be) is fashioned into suitable form, the divine Workman breathes the breath of life into his face and Man becomes a living person. The detail about the breath of life does not

[1] New York, Sheed & Ward, 1956.

denote what we call the "soul" (a term unknown as such to the Hebrews), for animals also have the "breath of life" (cf. Gen 7, 22; Job 34, 14ff.; Ps 104, 29ff.). Nonetheless, we can gather that Man is on a higher level than the animals both from this text (God's extraordinary care in producing Man) and from Man's later functions in the chapter, such as *naming* the animals and finding no one like himself among them. We may be sure that J entertains no debased notion of Man.

We must point out, too, that the first man is presented both as an individual and as *representative* of *all men.* To think in "totalities," or in what are often described as "corporate personalities," was a common practice among the Hebrews, where king, prophet, priest, and tribal founder or member represent an entire group (cf. Dt 18, 18). That is the case here. As we go through the story of Man, we (males) can see ourselves in him (as we are supposed to do), just as women can see themselves reflected in the portrait of Woman (later called Eve). This does not detract from the value of the account but enhances it. The very fact that J uses such a general name as Adam (Man) to describe the first man is already a strong hint at what he is trying to accomplish.

Gen 2, 7 cannot be employed as either for or against evolution. The whole concept of evolution was foreign to the writers of antiquity, and it is doubtful to the extreme that J gives us here anything like a rigorously objective description of how man was actually formed (something that he most probably knew nothing about). For this and other reasons, the volume of Ernesto Cardinal Ruffini, *The Theory of Evolution Judged by Reason and Faith*,[2] has not met with favor in the biblical world.

Pius XII very wisely laid down norms regarding evolution in his 1950 encyclical *Humani Generis, On Various Philosophical and Theological Errors,* giving it neither wholesale approval nor outright condemnation, but asking us not to accept hypotheses

---

[2] New York, Wagner, 1959. The Italian edition is considerably older.

for proved fact and demanding that we always admit the creation of the human soul by God. If there is anything that the recently published play (and movie) "Inherit the Wind" (based on the famous Scopes Trial of 1925) would teach us, it is the grave culpability and resulting damage of using the Bible as an anti-evolutionary and anti-scientific weapon. The slovenly and thoroughly blundering exegesis of J. Harrison Brady is such as to make us more ashamed of Scripture than anything else, and he is justly demolished by his adversary in the debate.

In Gen 2, 8 God becomes a Planter, for he is represented as making a marvellous garden *in* Eden, off towards the east. This garden is God's, not Man's. It is symbolic of divine life, or what we might term "the supernatural state," or "the state of original justice." The garden was planted out in the *steppe* region (the Babylonian word *edinu*, "steppe," probably underlies the Hebrew word *Eden*). The garden (translated in the Greek Bible as *parádeisos*, i.e. park (whence come our ideas of "paradise"), was situated "off to the east," a vague directive, denoting antiquity and mysteriousness. The "garden theme" was very ancient, taken over here by the J writer, but quite differently by Ezekiel in 28, 11–19.

Man's transferral to the garden signifies his elevation to the supernatural state, to wonderful divine friendship. This is the theological *reality* at which the writer is aiming.

Just as symbolic as the garden are the fine trees that it contains—all kinds of them, beautiful to look upon, providing abundant shade to the heat-oppressed orientals, and furnishing the choicest fruits. Two of the trees claim special attention. The first is the "tree of life" (common in Babylonian literature), symbolic of *immortality* and *grace*. The second is more mysterious. It is the "tree of the knowledge of good and evil." This refers to an experimental knowledge. To eat of its forbidden fruit would be the same as asserting moral autonomy, showing pride, and encroaching on God's sovereignty. It is the one tree from which

Man must not eat. This is a precept binding under penalty of losing the gift of immortality.

The four rivers spoken of in verses 10 to 14 are marked by a puzzling geography, for they all spring from one river as it passes through Eden. Rivers seldom divide in such manner; they rather converge. Moreover, while two of them are the Tigris and Euphrates, the other two seem to be situated in Arabia and Africa! These rivers are most likely intended to convey the ideal nature of the garden, and even the abundant grace available to man in his life of familiarity with God. The names of the rivers and places in these verses, as in the Canticle of Canticles, convey an air of mystery, romance, and fascination. The five verses could be omitted without disrupting the story in any way, though this does not prove that they are a later addition to the account.

Man's tasks in the garden are summed up by two verbs: to *work* it and to *guard* it. We need not press for details, such as "Guard it from what?" The terms are meant to tell us that Man is *entrusted* with something lofty, and that his work was a joy, not a drudgery.

In verse 18 the writer takes up the delicate question of sex. He makes his readers aware, first of all, of Man's loneliness; for God states: "It is not good for Man to be alone." Then God promises: "I will make for him a helpmate *corresponding to him*." The animal scene in verse 19 furthers the same idea, for Man found none of them to be of his nature. Let us recall that marriage in the Old Testament is always considered *normal*. Celibacy was unheard-of—at least for motives common within Christianity. Jeremiah practiced celibacy only to impress upon the people the inevitability and rapid approach of disaster.

In verse 21 God is presented as a surgeon. He casts a "deep sleep" upon Man; works secretly and mysteriously. From a "rib" of Man he forms Woman, Man's counterpart. God then presents the Woman to Man—as one presents a bride. Man is immediately attracted to her; his attention is thoroughly engaged and he heartily acknowledges Woman's equality with him: "Here now is bone of my bone; flesh of my flesh." He names the Woman *ishshah*, contrived as a feminine form of *'ish* (man). Thus while Man shows a certain leadership over Woman by naming her, he also acknowledges her equality of nature with him. Man is attracted to Woman. Love is born. This is something *God* has placed within the hearts of Man and Woman.

The J writer has a polemical motive in all this, too. He would like to see women, so often degraded and abused by men, loved, honored, and respected—as they should be.

We may suggest that the writer did not know, any more than we know, how Woman was actually formed. He is not writing a scientific treatise. He merely wants to show that Man is the exemplar of Woman, and in this sense she comes from him. This opinion has been advanced countless times by Catholic scholars and seems quite reconcilable with the 1909 decree of the Biblical Commission (where "formation of the first woman from the first man" must be held as a *fact*), especially in the light of the Suhard letter's invitation to fresh investigation of the literary form of this and other parts of Genesis.

Genesis offers a wholesome marriage ideal—one man and one woman clinging together for life, becoming two in one flesh. Flesh, by the way, does not denote in Hebrew thought merely the fleshy part of the body. It denotes the *entire person* under the aspect of *weakness*. The account, characterized throughout by an admirable tact and beauty, closes on the note of *innocence*. Man and Woman are unclad, yet feel no shame. This is tantamount to saying that passions, senses, reason—all within them—were in perfect harmony.

How long did such a condition go on? We have no way of knowing and the author has no intention of telling us, for he didn't know himself. We may leave Man and Woman here for the time being. They are friends of God; they are happy together—their state is ideal in every way. The stage, however, is set for a contest—a contest with evil. The J account merits very careful study and meditation. Try it yourself.

10 *GENESIS 3: MAN'S FALL FROM DIVINE FRIENDSHIP AND ITS CONSEQUENCES*

FEW CHAPTERS of the Bible are more important than the third chapter of Genesis. At the same time it is one of the most difficult to interpret. Much of what we will say is no more than opinion, even while it is opinion that has developed slowly and (we believe) solidly. No verse in the entire chapter has received a formal definition by the Church, though she has told us within certain limits what direction our interpretation should take. Not even the famous 3, 15—though figuring into a number of papal pronouncements—has been formally defined, as is evident from the guarded way in which popes have referred to this much-discussed text.

The entire chapter stems from the Yahwist (J) tradition, a tradition continuing right on from chapter 2 and running all the way through chapter 4. We must ask our readers to bear in mind what has already been said, for it is absolutely essential to what we are about to discuss. Most of chapter 2 served as a preparation and "stage setting" for the vital questions handled in chapter 3.

The peaceful scene with which chapter 2 closed is now disturbed by the appearance of "the serpent—the craftiest of all

the field-animals that God had made." This serpent is not specifically identified in our chapter, though his whole manner of
acting and speaking (!) shows that he is anti-God and out to
upset the wonderful relationship of Man and Woman with their
Maker, with each other, and with the rest of God's creation.
Other biblical passages, such as Wis 2, 24, Jn 8, 44 and Apoc 12,
9, leave no doubt that the serpent is the Devil. The story in its
most original form need not have been so explicit in its theology
on Satan—which developed only with time—yet the description
was never out of harmony with our present notions of Satan.

Here we must pose a question. Why should the Devil be presented as a serpent? Can we be satisfied with the explanation
that the serpent is among the most detested of animals and was
regarded as "wise," in the sense of "crafty" (Mt 10, 16)? Or is it
possible, as many scholars now believe, that since serpent figures,
representing fertility deities, were most probably used in the
illicit sex orgies carried out atop the Canaanite high places (at
the very time when our account was composed), the J writer
has chosen this image by way of polemic against these rites, ever
a pitfall for the Hebrew settlers? *This does not mean*, as we shall
take pains to point out further on, that the first sin was a sex
sin. It does mean that the sacred writer may have taken the
occasion to denounce the sex sins *of his own time*. This is quite
in harmony with the "reconstruction work" involved in the first
chapters of Genesis.

The wily serpent strikes up a conversation not with Man (who
appears to be "away") but with Woman (who seems to have
learned all about the rules of the Garden from Man—though she
quotes them in hyper-rigid form). One thing is sure. The serpent
is out to subvert God's authority. All his phrases are cleverly
couched in double-meanings, calling for sharp distinctions which
the Woman is not prepared to make or demand. It is not unlikely
that J, through this dialogue, is indicating that Woman is more
gullible than Man (in general, the Old Testament writers are

not too favorably disposed towards woman, cf. Qoheleth 7, 28 or Ben Sirah 25, 24).

The brief dialogue becomes more pointed all the time, ending in the serpent's outright denial of God's veracity ("You won't die at all") and the insinuation that God is simply jealous of the latent potentialities of Man and Woman, whose progress he is therefore holding in check—"God himself knows that on the day when you eat of that fruit your eyes will be opened; you will be like God; knowing good and evil." The statement is true—but in what a sorry sense! In only a few short phrases the Woman is completely shifted from her childlike obedience to a state of defiance and disobedience. The fruit of moral autonomy, of independence, of private decision, is attractive to the eyes, good to eat, and desirable "for acquiring understanding"—and so, Woman takes the fruit, eats of it, and then gives some to her mate who eats of it in turn.

Does the author wish to indicate anything to us by this ordering of events; that is, that Woman sins first, then Man? Probably he does. While J is far from being "anti-feminist," he is telling us that Woman is charming, that she may lead Man where he would not normally go—in short, that she may be a liability for Man (and this by no means signifies that Man is blameless!). Our author is interested in male-female relationships, and he makes a valuable point here.

Readers will look in vain for any mention of an "apple" here. The sacred text speaks of no more than "fruit." The "apple" idea, so prevalent in the popular mind, is taken over from Canticles 8, 5—from a text that was mistranslated in the Douay version, and then applied to the scene of Genesis that we are discussing.

The "originating sin" has been committed. What exactly was it? The J author really didn't know any more than we do. It is for that reason that he describes it in terms that apply to every serious sin; it is defiance; it is an assumption of the right to decide for oneself; it is pride; it is the transgression of a precept; it might possibly be associated with an inordinate desire for knowledge. Beyond this the writer could not go.

Was this a sex sin? If this refers to normal sex relations, the answer is absolutely negative, for Genesis favors *normal and licit* sex relations. As indicated above, the author may have *taken the occasion* to give vent to an indignant protest against the sex abuses so prevalent in his own time. In other words, there is a possible polemic involved here. Father Hubert Richards, Professor of Sacred Scripture at St. Edmund's, Ware, England, puts it thus: ". . . what the author of Genesis is pointing to as the root of all sin is not the use of the sexual faculties, but the deification of them, the making of them into an object of worship." That such was done in ancient Canaan is only too evident from the fertility figurines turned up in countless excavations, where the female organs of productivity and fertility are fantastically exaggerated.[1] Interested readers may find this question discussed at greater length in Fr. J. L. McKenzie's *The Two-Edged Sword*[2] or by Fr. B. J. LeFrois, S.V.D., in his article "The Forbidden Fruit" in *American Ecclesiastical Review*.[3]

The consequences of the first sin are frightful—even as described in the non-formal language of the Yahwist tradition. The eyes of Man and Woman are indeed opened, and they know that they are naked. Shame arises within them. They have been deceived. Their wholesome relationship with all about them—with God, with one another, with created things—is lost, and a horrible uneasiness results. In its formal language, the Council of Trent declares that it was "holiness and justice" that were lost (Denz., *Enchiridion Symbolorum*, No. 788). Man and Woman feel the need of clothing themselves and of hiding from

[1] Cf. W. F. Albright, *The Archaeology of Palestine* (Baltimore, Penguin Books, 1949), p. 107.

[2] Milwaukee, Bruce, 1956, pp. 90–108.

[3] 136 (March, 1957), pp. 175–83.

God, now depicted as a lord taking a late afternoon stroll through his garden.

The "trial scene" that follows is another expert piece of dialogue. The Lord calls to Man: "Where are you?" Far from discrediting the divine knowledge, this is simply a way of presenting a vivid and dramatic conversation. In just four searching, penetrating questions the Lord gets to the bottom of the entire affair. Each question is answered evasively, pushing the blame onto someone else—even onto God: "The woman that *you* gave me, it was she who gave me from the tree. . . ." Far from making fun of this account, we should recognize the real literary masterpiece that lies before us. It is filled with theological implications and conveys a tremendous *reality*. This is not allegory without foundation. As stated earlier, J's account is loaded with significance.

The culprits are penalized, beginning with the Tempter. He is cursed. He will crawl on his belly and eat dust. This does not mean that snakes began only at this time to slither along, body to earth—snakes always did that—but the snake's movements are now seen in a new light. The ancients believed, too, that snakes ate dust, for they *appeared* to do this. More seriously, the Devil and those linked with him will at some future time suffer a "crushing" defeat at the "heel" of the Woman and her seed. This is the heartening message of the "First Gospel" (Gen 3, 15), the first ray of hope offered to Man after the Fall. The text is obscure, and we cannot join hands with those that make of it a prodigy of theological content; yet the text does take on added significance *as the plan of redemption is unfolded.* The "woman" of the verse is none other than the Woman of the context—individual and representative, while her "seed" is mankind, sprung from her.

In the "fuller sense" (that known to God, but *not* to the human inspired writer at the time of writing), the one Man who will achieve victory over the Devil is Christ, and he will be born of a spotless Virgin—the greatest Woman of all time. This is but one way of explaining the text, one which is quite in harmony with papal directives, as far as they go.

Man and Woman both are to suffer in their *essential* offices: Woman as mother and wife; Man as worker. Woman, having lost her right relationship with God, loses also her ability to face her tasks of wife and mother with calm and reason. And, though often maltreated by Man, she will nonetheless be unfailingly attracted to him, just as it is Man's weakness that he is unfailingly drawn to her.

Neither Man nor Woman is cursed, but the earth is, and Man's labor is henceforth to be painful drudgery. The earth will not respond to his efforts, and he, made from the clay of the earth (2, 7), will one day return to it—the J writer's way of saying that Man has lost the preternatural gift of immortality. It is with these sober words of Gen 3, 19 that the Church admonishes her children on Ash Wednesday.

It is noteworthy that the earth is only cursed with respect to Man, not in itself. The material universe, with all its forms of life, was only abased through the Fall insofar as Man lost his right relationship to God's marvellous creation. The universe is actually now just as it was before the time of the Fall—but Man has changed. It is the work of Redemption gradually to restore Man to a proper relationship with everything about him. The Hebrews readily associated all creation with man—for man is its lord. Checking a passage like Is 33, 9 will help us get a more exact idea of our section of Genesis, for there nature withers as Sennacherib approaches.

Man's dominion over Woman is demonstrated in a verse (20) that has all the earmarks of being out of place. Here Man names Woman Eve (in Hebrew Hawwah), the name being derived from the verb *hawah*, i.e. "to live," and the name Eve is said to mean "mother of all that lives." This seems to anticipate the events of chapter 4.

A kindly act, showing that he has not utterly rejected Man, is performed by Yahweh in verse 21. He makes clothing for Man and Woman, and even clothes them! Man, however, may never again have the opportunity of tasting of the tree of life and thus regaining immortality. No, he must be cast forth from the Garden of God, from familiarity with God, and gain his livelihood on a harsher terrain. All possibility of re-entrance is cut off by the posting of "cherubim" and a "flaming, whirling sword" to prevent access to the Garden and to the tree of life. The "cherubim" (*keribi*) found at the gates of Babylonian temples as well as the flaming sword are images borrowed from other peoples of the ancient Near East. Of the flaming sword Canon Albert Clamer, in his commentary on Genesis, says: "Assyro-Babylonian analogies allow us to represent this flame as zigzag lightning between the cherubim."[4]

Genesis does not go into the question of "original sin" though it does deal with those hereditary penalties that afflict all mankind and which are *signs* of original sin. It is only with St. Paul (Rom 5) that the doctrine of original sin is brought into full focus.

Undoubtedly bound up with the narrative that we have been discussing is the Hebrew concept of "corporate personality," a term first popularized by H. Wheeler Robinson less than a hundred years ago, and now standard biblical terminology. This concept implies that individuals were viewed by the Hebrews not in isolated fashion but as members of a society or clan, as descendant from, or representative of, a larger group. It is thus that Adam, with some fluidity, is both one and mankind, and that his sin afflicts not merely himself but all those identified with him. Readers will note that we have rather studiously avoided the terms "Adam" and "Eve." Our purpose was precisely to try to convey something of the Hebrew writer's mentality as he collectivized mankind in one Man.

[4] *Genèse* (Paris, Letouzey et Ané, 1953).

Chapter 3 of Genesis is one of the greatest writings of all times. Placed in its real literary setting and properly understood, it has an unmatched genius. It is simple, almost parabolic, highly dramatic, yet a deeply theological presentation of an extremely difficult and delicate subject. Basically it is an explanation of the *condition of mankind*. The chapter has many subtleties of language and thought that we have not touched upon. These can be found in lengthier commentaries by those wishing to go into the matter more thoroughly. Of great help will be the study by Hauret to which we have already referred, *Beginnings*, as well as *A Path Through Genesis* by Father Vawter. Above all, read the chapter itself; think about it; weigh it. Let its lessons sink in deeply.

11 BEFORE THE FLOOD: GENESIS 4–5

THE FIRST ELEVEN CHAPTERS of Genesis, while offering a surprising variety of materials, are built around a simple plan. Dealing *generally* with the origins of the world and of mankind, three major sections may be discerned: (1) Creation and Fall (1, 1—6, 4); (2) the Flood (6, 5—9, 17); and (3) from the Flood to Abraham (9, 18—11, 32). What we find in chapters 4 and 5, therefore, belongs to the first section, and, more specifically, demonstrates the consequences of sin—consequences which at the same time are the causes of the Flood; for the Flood is always considered in the Bible as a punishment for the utter depravity of mankind.

While chapter 4 springs from the Yahwist (J) tradition, chapter 5 belongs to the Priestly (P) tradition, both chapters having the same general lesson to convey, but each in its own way. While J presents, in keeping with its bent, concrete examples of man's sinfulness, P will put across the same lesson through a cleverly constructed and synchronized genealogy, freighted with meaning. Both writers are preparing us for the Flood, the great watershed (!) within the first eleven chapters of Genesis. Let us see what these traditions have to tell us, always looking for religious and not scientific instruction.

Genesis 4: the Yahwist Account

The J writer in chapter 4 presents what we might call an anecdotal genealogy, for he attaches interesting stories to most of the characters he introduces. The terms "Adam" and "Eve" are now given a singularized meaning, for the couple enter upon their task of "increasing and multiplying." Two sons are born to them, Cain, the elder, who takes up truck-gardening, and Abel, the younger, a shepherd. Here, as in many other places in the Old Testament, two ways of life, the sedentary and nomadic, are contrasted, and the nomadic is given the odds. Too, the elder son is rejected by God in favor of the younger (note later on in Genesis the stories of Jacob and Esau, or of Ephraim and Manasseh).

Cain and Abel both offer sacrifice, each after his own manner of life, and it is Abel's sacrifice that finds favor with God. Genesis does not tell us why, though a reason is assigned in Heb 11, 4. The J writer is probably stressing the superiority of nomadism, for one thing. Cain's murder of Abel is a horribly brutal act, showing the fruits of jealousy, and his sullen dishonesty with God, when interrogated, only piles sin upon sin. We must not pass over Cain's lament in 4, 13ff., discon-

certing as it may be. Cain states that whoever encounters him
will kill him. Yet, were we to take a strictly historical approach
to this account, we could point to no more than three people
then existing, Adam, Eve, and Cain. This alerts us to something very important in this chapter, namely, that there are
a number of signs indicating that Cain and his progeny are
situated in an already advanced civilization: the earth is
populated, the crafts are known, cities are being built (Cain's
own son builds a city!), metals are in use, and so on. Again,
there is the classical query: Where did Cain find a wife? Genesis
does not tell us, but there are plenty of hints that he found
her among the *many* people that were in existence at that time.
We can hardly escape the conclusion that the J writer has
taken the oldest genealogy that he could find and has simply
attached it to First Man and First Woman, thus bringing about
a continuity, but one that is highly artificial.

There are so many seams in this presentation that the observant
reader can readily perceive what has been done. Note, too,
the clan mark given to Cain, lest he be killed by those of other
clans (for clans avenged, and still avenge, the murder of one
of their members). If the reader will take the trouble to assemble the genealogy found in chapter 4 and place it alongside that of chapter 5, he will also notice some most interesting
features: that many of the names are exactly the same, others
almost the same, but that the ordering is at times different—
showing that J and P were working with different sources.

Thus we are forced to the conclusion that these writers are
presenting genealogies that were neither rigidly historical nor
chronological, despite appearances. This does not mean that
the writers meant to deceive their readers. It does mean that
they (and the final editor of Genesis) simply used the information at hand in order to convey through it lessons *other*
than those of science, history, and chronology.

To add to his illustration of sin's rampage, J introduces

Lamech in 4, 18, a swaggering, uncouth bigamist. His spirit of vengeance goes far beyond the ordinary Hebrew law of "an eye for an eye and a tooth for a tooth" (which was really a mitigation of the generally harsher attitudes of other peoples), and his sons, with their strange and indicative names of Jabal (guider), Jubal (musician), and Tubal-cain (smith) are all professional men (herdsman, minstrel, and metal-worker, respectively). It is of interest that the Bronze Age in Palestine began around 3000 B.C. and the Iron Age around 1200 B.C. This would bring Tubal-cain down to a relatively late age in the history of mankind, and again reveals the artificial character of the genealogy.

While these men and women receive Hebrew names, it is certain that Hebrew was not the oldest of languages. Actually, it is rather a latecomer on the language scene. The etymologies, too, are nearly all what may be called "popular," not based on scientific philology. Thus the name Cain (Hebrew: Qain) in 4, 1 is said to derive from the verb *qanah* and would mean "I have acquired (a man)." Such etymologies remind us of the quaint Latin etymologies of Isidore of Seville, most of them without solid foundation. Yet Hebrews, like other peoples, loved these word-plays, and the etymologies have their own lesson to convey.

Towards the end of chapter 4, Adam begets other children from Eve—information that comes from a separate ancient tradition—and Seth is born, who in turn begets Enoch. Note the very different positions of these men in the genealogy of chapter 5. Seth, a man of piety, begins to call on the name of Yahweh—a name revealed to Moses at a much later date, according to Exod 6, 3ff., but used here perhaps by anticipation. It is this freer use of the name Yahweh which, as we saw earlier, caused this tradition to be designated as "Yahwist."

There is no need to be shocked by these peculiarities of the J writer. He accomplishes the purposes that he had in mind

quite admirably, even though his methods are very far removed from our own. To disguise them would be a fault on
our part. We must face them honestly and squarely, realizing
that, judged by the writing standards of those times, they do
not mar what we hold as an article of faith, i.e. the errorless-
ness of the Bible. This would be a good place to refer back to
our remarks on this subject in chapter 3. We can see why inerrancy was known in the nineteenth century as *the* Biblical
question.

Genesis 5: the Priestly Account

The P. account beginning with chapter 5 may be attached
directly to Gen 2, 4a (where P left off). Try reading 5, 1ff.
right after 2, 4a. P takes us, without a "Fall" story, from First
Man right up to the Flood, accomplishing roughly the same
purpose that J accomplishes in chapter 4. P's ten-entry genealogy
(corresponding to the ten-entry post-Flood genealogy by the
same P writer in Gen 11, 10–32), carries us over the long time-
span from First Man to the Flood. The ten-entry structure on
either side of the Flood is ample evidence of artificiality and
mnemonics.

Despite sin, God's image in Man was never lost (as we see in
Gen 5, 1–3), for it is a quality inherent in Man's nature—a
sharing in God's dominion over created things lower than Man.
Grace, however, helps us to employ this endowment correctly.

Readers will quickly note the arithmetical character of
chapter 5—it is filled with numbers, and the numbers are *large*.
We find some of these early patriarchs living fabulously long
lives—all the way up to 969 years (Methuselah)! The numbers
were certainly intended by the P writer to be high, even though
they are in some cases imperfectly transmitted to us (as a

comparison of the Massoretic, Septuagint, and Samaritan data will readily reveal).

Many generations of Bible readers have wondered how these patriarchs managed to live such long lives. Our answer today can only be: they didn't. Scientific studies of early man show that he actually lived a shorter life than we live today.

The discovery of the ancient Babylonian king lists during the last century has also alerted us to another approach to the question. In these lists we find the *regnal* years of the Babylonian rules reaching astronomical figures such as 72,000 years (Enmeduranna of Sippar). One of the lower figures is a mere 10,800 years. Such figures makes those of Gen 5 pale into near insignificance. Yet they guide us in interpreting these biblical numbers. We are at least aware that the ancient orientals indicated something special by their figures, something other than the face value that we so often attribute to them today. That this is the correct *approach* few Catholic biblical scholars would doubt.

But what is meant by such a high life-span as 969 years? It has been suggested that the figures are inflated in order to fill in what the P writer surmised was a big time-gap between the First Man and the Flood. While this is not unreasonable, still it is interesting to total up the years that are actually filled in, and it will be found surprisingly small. The reason for this is that each patriarch begets his principal offspring long before he arrives at anything near his full age, and for that reason the *total* number of years spanned between Adam's death and the Flood is not large—something like 956 years! This is really a very small figure when we consider the many millennia that man has actually been on earth.

Another suggestion is that the large figures attached to each patriarch would indicate to the reader, not how long man actually lived on earth but how long *ago*. Big numbers are impressive, even today, and we are not above using them to put over a point.

There seems to be something much deeper, however, in the use of these high figures. A partial answer may well lie in the steady decrease in age-lengths of the patriarchs as we go forth in the book of Genesis. When we say "steady," we do not mean that *each* patriarch lives less years than his predecessor, but rather that the tendency is steadily towards shorter lives until they become nearly "normal" by the end of the book. What would this indicate?

The Hebrews had a very hazy notion of the future life. Throughout nearly the whole of the Old Testament, their belief is summed up in the word "Sheol," almost synonymous with "the grave." It was a kind of survival, beneath the earth, yet hardly a thing to look forward to. In Sheol man could not praise God; he could not find happiness; it was a kind of amorphous, clouded, weakened existence (cf. Is 14, 9ff.; Ps 88 [89], 4ff.). The best thing was to live on earth as long as possible. It was a common belief that the just were *kept* on earth longer than the unjust. This is undoubtedly the meaning of the psalm verse: "Costly in the eyes of the Lord is the death of his saints" (Ps 116, 15), for God does not wish to break the bonds of love and praise that unite him and his holy ones *on earth*—but these bonds are broken if they descend to Sheol. Hence the Priestly writer, by gradually lessening man's earthly life-span, shows that sin was atomizing mankind and gradually gaining the ascendancy. According to Is 65, 20 a long life (the equivalent of sinlessness) would be one of the marks of the messianic age.

Such an explanation has much in its favor, though it does not exhaust the numerical philosophy of the Priestly writer. The 365 years of Enoch (based on the number of days in a solar year) are certainly meant to bring out his perfect life (that is why God "took" him), and if you figure out the mathematics of Methuselah's life-span with relation to his progeny, you will discover the interesting fact that he died the very year the

Flood occurred—perhaps an indication that his goodness of life (indicated by his 969 years) brought him to the grave *just before* the Flood.

These numbers, at all events, must be judged by standards other than our own of today. They are part of a clever construction, the secrets of which have not been, and probably never will be, fathomed (since they have suffered to some extent in transmission). Nonetheless, we are not utterly at a loss in handling them, and the indications given above will at least put us on the right track.

Genesis 6, 1–4: The Sons of God and the Daughters of Men

A final illustration from the Yahwist tradition is inserted into the Genesis account before the Flood story proper. It is an account, which we can only describe as legendary, of a group of pre-Flood giants—physically huge but morally puny. These giants were the offspring of male "angels" and female human beings. As ridiculous as this sounds, there were many such stories among the ancients (compare the Greek Titans). The story is not inserted here because it was accepted by the inspired writer as objectively true, but rather because it served as an *illustration* of the type of moral corruption that brought on the Flood. According to the J author (and here he is quite out of harmony with P's system), man will henceforth live no longer than 120 years on earth. While J and P agree in their philosophy of longevity, their expression of it is not numerically the same, for P will concede more than 120 years of life to his post-Flood patriarchs (Gen 11, 10–32).

Those who are sceptical about the "angels-women" interpretation mentioned above may be interested to know that it is the most ancient Jewish and Christian interpretation of this difficult passage, and that it was only a refined notion of angels that caused later Church Fathers to abandon it. Even in our days, certain orientals believe that spirits (jinns) can bring about human conception! This is illustrated by a number of incidents in Père Jaussen's famous book on Palestinian customs.[1]

If there is any lesson that these pre-Flood accounts bring out, it is that sin is man's greatest enemy, and that it must be punished by God, who is both merciful and just.

12 NOAH, HIS ARK, AND THE FLOOD

CENTRALLY SITUATED (6, 5—9, 17) in the first eleven chapters of Genesis is the story of the Flood. We have been prepared for it by chapters 4, 1 to 6, 4, where sin's increasing grip on man was illustrated by both the Yahwist and Priestly traditions. Arrogant, defiant, blinded and deeply corrupted, man must be punished. The Flood will serve as God's agent, "blotting out" not only man but also other sectors of creation associated with him—animals, birds, and other living or non-living creatures. Only a select remnant will be spared, with an eye to a new beginning. That the Bible presents the Flood as a consequence of moral guilt is so evident that there is no need to dwell on the point.

As already stated several times, it is absolutely imperative for a full understanding of Genesis to recognize the various and

[1] A. Jaussen, O.P., *Coutumes palestiniennes* (Paris, Guethner, 1927), Vol. I, pp. 230–34.

variant traditions that have gone into it. Hence, though our
readers may grow weary of it, we cannot help referring to J
(Yahwist tradition or writer) and P (Priestly tradition or
writer). To neglect this would be disastrous for an objective and
satisfying exposition of the book.

As strange as it may seem, Genesis really presents *two* Flood
stories, one according to J, which is more colorful and lively
(God is "sorry" that he made man; God *closes* the door of the
Ark when all are safely inside!); the other according to P, which
is better thought-out, more reflective and "dry." There are several commentaries that present the stories separately, so that
readers can see for themselves how *nearly complete* each story is
and also note the differences between them. Thus Prof. Gerhard
von Rad of Göttingen[1] treats first J and then P, while Abbé
Joseph Chaine[2] places the two accounts in parallel columns so
that readers can make their comparison with the least amount
of effort. That the final editor of Genesis has woven these two
accounts together with considerable dexterity and yet without
appreciably altering either story is ample evidence for the peculiar "historical" methodology of ancient Near Eastern writers.
They obviously had great respect for tradition—to such a degree that they preferred to present two or more variant versions
of the same incident rather than decide (by critical methods,
which were foreign to them) which one was correct.

Before going any further, we must once more bring an old
issue to the fore. Some (of various faiths) remain adamant in
taking everything in these accounts in a rigorously literal sense,
maintaining that the Bible means exactly what it says, no matter
what science or scientific exegesis might suggest. This is *funda-
mentalism,* a procedure almost entirely abandoned by Catholic
scholarship for a number of reasons and with the approbation
and guidance of the Church herself. What we have said about

---

[1] *Das erste Buch Mose, Genesis* (Göttingen, 1958), pp. 53–92.
[2] *Le Livre de la Genèse* (Paris, Editions du Cerf, 1951), pp. 114–22.

two variant accounts is already sufficient reason to put us on our guard against it. There are variations in the number of animals taken into the Ark, in the source of the Flood waters, in the entire chronology of the Flood, etc. But even more, the discovery of other Flood accounts, the findings of science, the literary methods of the ancients (especially hyperbole: exaggeration for effect), and the highly dramatic write-up—all lead us in another direction in our evaluation of the Flood accounts of Genesis. In dealing with Genesis (and other sections of the Bible) we have come to learn an important fact: it is not so much history (in our rigid sense of the term) that is at issue, as the *eternal and dynamic lessons* conveyed through the presentation of historical or non-historical events.

I have no intention of questioning the basic historicity of the Flood, of Noah, or of the Ark, but I insist that both J and P, as well as the final editor of their accounts, were interested in conveying *lessons* rather than historical detail. This is a most important distinction, the *misunderstanding* of which has brought discredit to the Bible and at the same time has caused some people of the very best will unjustly to condemn modern biblical scholars as having denied the historicity of various biblical events. All that scholars have done is to make an attempt at evaluating the *meaning* of the Bible; they have attempted to place the emphasis where it belongs—not on historical detail but on the instructional efforts of the inspired writers.

The vast Mesopotamian (Babylonian) region knew *several* floods in ancient times. This is evidenced by geological tests and by the flood stories that were written up by the ancient Babylonians and Sumerians. These ancient accounts, e.g. the Gilgamesh Epic, especially Tablet Eleven,[3] display remarkable similarities to the biblical flood stories, although they are much inferior in theological conception. There is no question of the Bible having borrowed its material from them. It is more likely

[3] Cf. Pritchard, *op. cit.*, pp. 65–75.

that both biblical writers and the Babylonians drew on common sources.

At the risk of incurring the displeasure of our readers, we must insist that there were several ancient Babylonian floods of a serious nature; that one of these floods was described in especially hyperbolized language; that the description took on cosmic and universal aspects even though the flood so described was actually local—though serious; and that *this* is the Flood spoken of in the Bible. This means, coming down to concrete terms, that the biblical Flood *neither* covered the entire earth *nor* did it blot out all men.

The statement is sometimes made that a flood tradition is common over the entire earth. This is simply not true. John E. Steinmueller, a scholar noted for his conservatism and a consultor of the Biblical Commission, has this to say on the matter: "In profane literature the tradition of the flood is not universal. Though unknown to the Egyptians, most Indo-European races, the Arabs, the Chinese and the Japanese, it has survived among the Greeks, Polynesians, American Indians, and in particular among the Babylonians."[4] What, too, were once thought to be flood remains in various strata of the earth have turned out to be the results of gigantic glaciers. This matter is taken up in considerable detail by F. Ceuppens, O.P.[5]

Since there is evidence in the Mesopotamian area of more than one flood, it is almost impossible to venture a date for the Flood spoken of in Genesis. Since, however, the Sumerian account goes back to something like 2000 B.C., we may suggest that the biblical Flood may have occurred some four thousand years ago. André Parrot, a famous archaeologist and the curator of the Oriental section of the Louvre, would even raise the figure to some five thousand years ago.

Now to get back to the question of the universality of the

[4] *Companion to the Old Testament* (New York, Wagner, 1946), p. 78.
[5] *Quaestiones ex Historia Primaeva* (Rome, 1947), pp. 320–21.

Flood. If we had the childlike, simple concept of the universe that the ancient orientals had, where the earth was thought of as nearly flat (the mountains being caused by the protruding "pillars" upon which the earth rested), and as much more restricted in area than we know it is today, a "world" flood would not be so difficult to imagine. With our modern (and authentic) conception of the earth and universe, such a coverage of the earth by flood waters is out of the question—not to speak of other factors such as inducing, as Father Vawter observes, representatives of the "519,000 distinct species of living creatures"[6] to enter the Ark, or of accounting for languages among men today that have taken millennia to develop. Here it is not a mark of "faith" or of loyalty to the Church to be fundamentalist. We must strain every nerve to get to the bottom of the meaning of the Flood accounts, and this leads us not to an outright denial of the historicity of the Flood and the factors involved in it, but to an evaluation of the biblical accounts. In doing this, we are doing exactly what the Church has asked us to do—we are using our God-given reason to understand the inspired Word of God. To do otherwise is to do a disservice to authentic religion and to widen the rift that has *unnecessarily* separated religion and science in many minds.

The hero of the Flood is a man named Noah. Where corruption reigned, Noah proved himself just, and for that reason was selected as a recipient of the divine mercy. With him were his wife, his three sons and their wives. These, together with whatever animals and birds were brought into the Ark, were to be the source of a "new beginning" (in that part of the world). It was in his five hundredth year that Noah begot his three sons, Ham, Shem, and Japheth, and it was in his six hundredth year that the Flood occurred. In none of these matters could we afford to press for the historicity of details, though there is no reason to question the general historicity of the event. The two figures

6 *A Path Through Genesis,* p. 88.

"five hundred" and "six hundred" hardly bear an ordinary numerical value. In these matters it is very difficult to draw the delicate line that divides the historical from the symbolic.

The word used for "ark" in Hebrew is *tebah*—the same word used in Exod 2, 3 to describe the "basket" in which the infant Moses was placed and set adrift on the Nile. The word comparison is interesting, for in both cases protection is given, and in both instances pitch or resin was used to make the vessels waterproof. The term itself means simply a box or chest. Whatever the Ark was, it was assuredly not the launch or liner-like structure so often depicted. The Ark was not intended for cruising purposes. It had the simple duty of lifting its occupants up upon the Flood waters and later on, when the waters had subsided, of lowering them down once more to the earth. The dimensions presented in the Bible, 450' by 75' by 45', are very likely exaggerated, though they are not utterly impossible. Even allowing for the simplest construction plans, it would have been a prodigious task for Noah to build such an Ark.

Will the Ark be discovered in our days? Those who followed the press on this subject during the summer of 1960 will recall the investigations of a "boat-like object" (with sharp bow and stern) which were made in early June at 7,000-foot level near Mt. Ararat. No evidence could be found that the earthen formation was man-made. Rather it seemed to be the result of a landslide, though the *Life Magazine* report did mention small chunks of wood that were turned up through dynamiting. The American team's report on their investigations was not enthusiastic, nor did biblical experts think that it would be.

As mentioned above, the importance of the Flood accounts lies not in rigid historicity, but in the eternal lessons linked to these accounts. Thus a strong lesson in God's justice is provided —but also the less difficult lesson of God's mercy to those who serve him, and even to mankind in general (post-Flood events). The reader is meant also to grasp something of the horror of human malice. Hebrews 11, 7 sees a lesson in Noah's "faith, whereby he condemned the world, and became an heir of a justice based on faith." Our Lord's discourse on Jerusalem's destruction—exemplifying final judgment—mentions the Flood as a foretaste of swift and unexpected judgment (Lk 17, 26ff.; Mt. 24, 37ff.).

St. Peter (1 Pet 3, 20–21) derives still another lesson from the Flood waters. He sees in them a foreshadowing of baptism, for, just as Noah and his family were *saved* by the Flood waters (as they lifted the Ark aloft), so is the Christian saved through the waters of baptism. Early Christians saw the Ark itself as a foreshadowing of the Church—the only means of salvation (deliverance) from the divine anger. Here are the everlasting lessons of the Flood, those that should preoccupy us first and foremost.

Did the Flood achieve its purpose? If by this we mean that mankind began a new way of life—no longer dominated by sin —we will have to answer in the negative. Gen 8, 21, part of a soliloquy placed in the "mouth" of God, would give the lie to any other answer. Here, rather, God's plan of dealing with man is altered: "I will never again destroy every living creature, as I have done." The lesson that the author will convey is one of God's patience and mercy with us. If the above-stated question means: Did the Flood *accounts* achieve their purpose? we may answer affirmatively. The story is well presented and should deeply impress its readers and win them to a more loyal service of God.

After the Flood, God enters into a Covenant with Noah and mankind. The Covenant is one of mercy. Never again will God deal with man *according to man's guilt.* Were God to do so, it would mean the destruction of us all. Whenever we see the rainbow in the sky, we are to think of this. Disasters there may be; great sorrows there may be; tragedies there may be—and our age is the witness to plenty of them: yet if the Covenant with Noah means anything, it means that God is only punishing us part-measure. This rule, however, is a general rule and is hardly meant to explain (at least to our complete satisfaction) every concrete and particular instance of human sorrow and tragedy.

The post-Flood account makes a concession to human weakness. Man may now eat meat. The meat that man eats, however, must have the blood drained from it, for blood, as the ancients thought, was the seat of life—and hence sacred to God. Blood, so important in sealing the Israelite Covenant (Exod 24, 6ff.), was also used in various expiation rites. Our own redemption was partly achieved through Christ's shedding of his blood, but also through his glorious resurrection—this latter aspect being so often neglected.

It is clear from what follows upon the Flood stories that man continues in sin. Man's abuse of God's tolerant goodness will have much to do with the course that the Old and New Testaments take—not to speak of salvation history going on right now.

We have been unable to touch on many finer details of the Flood traditions; but what we have said will show how the sacred writers have given an everlasting meaning to one of many ancient floods in the Mesopotamian region.

13 FROM THE FLOOD TO ABRAHAM

IN JUST two and a half chapters the book of Genesis is going to leap across another great time-gap—from the Flood to Abraham (Gen 9, 18 to 11, 32). It is this section that we now propose to examine, and some very important and interesting materials await our attention: the Curse upon Canaan; the Table of Nations; the Tower of Babel; and another Priestly genealogy. We may as well gird our loins for some unusual presentations—"literary forms" that are far removed from our modern ways of writing and thinking, as the ancient writers look more to lessons than to objective history.

It is the Yahwist tradition (noted, you will recall, for its colorful and chatty stories) that offers a not-too-easy-to-fathom narrative about Noah, his sons, winemaking, family decency, and the curse hurled at Canaan. Let us see what we can make of it.

When the Flood was over, Noah took up vinedressing. The wording of chapter 9, verse 18, seems to ignore all that has occurred since 8, 18. We are here informed that the entire earth was repeopled by Noah's sons—Canaan, son of Ham, now coming in for special mention. Actually, Noah's sons are looked upon as the ancestors of ethnic groups, the Canaanites being linked to the Hamites (see below). Their repeopling of the earth is regarded as the result of the powerful blessing imparted to them by Yahweh (cf. 9, 1ff.).

Noah's unintended inebriation need not in itself raise a moral issue. The fact that he had enough presence of mind to get into his tent makes this even more true. Palestine and adjacent regions have long been famous for their choice and *potent* wines. Hints of this are discernible in Is 16, 8–10, where the heady wines of Moab are mentioned; and in Ez 27, 18, where there is question of the wine of Helbon (north of Damascus), brought into Tyre.

Gen 9, 22 indicates guilt on Ham's part, at least for looking indiscreetly upon his father lying unclad within his tent. Good Hebrews were very sensitive on this point (cf. Dt 27, 16). The modesty of Shem and Japheth is shown by their almost ridiculous solicitude—walking backward with a cloak to throw over their father.

Readers of this section note that the whole guilt is suddenly thrown onto Canaan when Noah awakes. Even if we have been somewhat prepared for this strange course of events by the Yahwist's care always to mention Ham *as the father of Canaan*, still we note some peculiarities in the account. Ham is called the *youngest* son in 9, 24, yet all previous registers would give this position to Japheth. But, more especially, the reader may well query, What did Canaan *do* to merit the dire curse that fell upon him from the lips of the irate Noah, and how did Noah "know" that Canaan was guilty of what the text attributes to Ham? The text, as we have it, has certainly been troubled by additions or subtractions, Canaan perhaps at one time having been listed as the son of Noah in place of Ham. It is not out of the question that the writer wishes to imply that Canaan committed a sin of sodomy with Noah, something comparable to the act of Lot's daughters in Gen 19. One thing is certain. This account is aimed directly against the Canaan of the writer's own time, just as Gen 19 deals a decidedly low blow against the Ammonites and Moabites; just as Ben Sirah speaks of the people of Seir, Philistia, and Samaria as "detested" and "stupid" (51, 25–26, or in another enumeration of verses, 27–28); just as Nathanael wonders if anything worthwhile could come out of such a disreputable place as Nazareth (Jn 1, 46); and just as Paul endorses the harsh statements of Epimenides about the Cretans: "The men of Crete were ever liars, venomous creatures, all hungry belly and nothing besides; and that is a true account of them" (Tit 1, 12–13, Knox). That the Hebrews were capable of a loathing detestation for their enemies, especially for the immoral, licentious Canaanites, goes without saying. We have already had a good sampling of this in the serpent polemic of chapter 3, and those who read their Bible will find plenty of additional material —nor should we omit mention of the imprecatory psalms! (Try Ps 109 [108] for instance.) After all, the Hebrews were God's chosen people, and those who served as a snare to them could hardly expect a blessing—not in those times.

Though a curse may roll off us and soon be forgotten, it was not so with the ancient Semites. Curses and blessings were very serious affairs, considered to have permanent effects, as the stories of Jacob and Esau vying for Isaac's blessing (Gen 27) and the summoning of Balaam by Balak (Num 22—24) amply illustrate. Here, as clouded as the incident may otherwise be, the Yahwist writer pours out all his venom on the Canaanites, immoral sodomites if there ever were such (see Gen 19, 1ff.). That he felt even the slightest prick of conscience in speaking this way about the Canaanites seems quite unlikely.

While Ham and Canaan are "painted in the darkest colors" (approximate words of Martin Luther), an expression which furthered the utterly ridiculous and truly accursed notion that Ham (or Canaan) was father of the colored people,[1] Noah blesses Yahweh, the God of the Semites (represented by Shem), whose slave Canaan (i.e. the Canaanites) is to be. The statement regarding Japheth is not as easy to interpret as it is to translate: "May God make room (*yaphet*) for Japheth ("Yepheth"—a Hebrew pun), and may he dwell in the tents of Shem!" This seems to point to peaceful co-dwelling of Japhethites (cf. Gen 10, 2–5) with the S(h)emites, even to the sharing of the latters' religion. The descendants of Shem, the Semites, especially the Hebrews, are to find their greatness in blessing Yahweh, the one true God.

The final verses of this chapter give us a total of Noah's years —no less than 950—to be interpreted along the lines pointed out in chapter 11. Such a high number should allay any suspicions regarding his justice, for he lags only nineteen years behind the record-breaking Methuselah.

[1] Cf. Lawrence Friedel, S.V.D., in *American Ecclesiastical Review*, 106 (1942), pp. 447–53, where this question is capably discussed.

Chapter 10 of Genesis is usually called the *Table of Nations*. It is taken mostly from the P tradition with little sprinklings of J here and there. Thus we find several contradictions within the chapter, e.g. v. 7 as against vv. 26–29. While built in the form of a genealogical table, tracing the descendants of Noah, the chapter is something of an ethnic chart, showing less of blood relationship than of geographical, historical, and even commercial data. The account, though based on ideas current at the time of the writer, is astoundingly objective insofar as Israel is omitted from the scene completely—for "it is a people destined to dwell apart, not counted among the muster-roll of the nations" (Num 23, 9, Knox). P, too, is insistent, as in chapter 1, that God's influence and blessing (cf. 10, 32 and 9, 1) lie behind all nations and peoples, all human society.

Whatever else this chapter is, *it is not scientific ethnology*. The Japhethites (mostly friends of the Semites) are made up of inhabitants of Asia Minor and the Mediterranean Isles; the Hamites inhabit the southern lands, especially Egypt, Ethiopia, Arabia, and (!!) Canaan. The Semites lie in between these two groups, and comprise Elamites, Assyrians, Aramaeans, and the Hebrew forefathers—sons of Eber. The chapter, with its limited geographical horizons, sets forth ideas that were common around the time of Solomon (961–922, [Albright dating]). We must not fail to point out that P already distinguishes men according to language (10, 5. 20. 31), though J, in chapter 11, operates under a different assumption. While some of the descendants mentioned in this chapter, like the famous huntsman Nimrod, may have been individuals, most of the names are those of peoples or cities. This is comparable to stating that Great Britain begot the United States. Yet, despite scientific deficiencies, our chapter is not bereft of value. As the illustrious Joseph Chaine stated: "The author has a great outlook on the common origin of all men; and, going through the maze of peoples, he traces out the plan of

God who was about to elect one tribe and make preparation for its rise."[2]

Chapter 11 opens with the story of the Tower and City of Babel (perhaps once two separate stories), related from the Yahwist tradition. The assumption is that mankind spoke one language: "All the earth was one lip and the same words" (a slavish translation of the Hebrew text). There are many questions that we may ask about this narrative. Why is it situated *here* by the editor of Genesis? How historical is it? What is its chief purpose? Let us venture some answers.

The story is most probably situated here since, on the one hand, time had to be given (through chapter 10) for mankind to develop after the Flood (we note a *migration* in our story), and since, on the other hand, the editor wished to take up the genealogy of Shem next, and this would bring him right up to Abraham, the story could not be postponed. Hence, though involving not a few disadvantages, this was the best place to present the Yahwist story. To compare it chronologically with the Table in chapter 10 is most difficult, even though "Babel" is spoken of in 10, 10. The traditions are obviously quite independent of one another, nor does the editor make much effort to bring them into harmony. He includes them as the best information he can get to fill in this sparsely documented period of pre-Hebrew history.

That this Babel story has an historical kernel we need not deny, especially since the ziggurats, grandiose step-like towers of astounding proportions built by Mesopotamian monarchs in honor of the astral deities, have been discovered—the first "skyscrapers." Nebuchadnezzar built one at Borsippa, and the materials spoken of in Gen 11, 3 were actually used in the ziggurats. However, the story is mostly fictional in its present form, a fact which does not in the least impair its high didactic value.

As the account now stands, its main lesson is this: works

[2] *Op. cit.*, p. 159.

undertaken in defiance of God and for purposes of pride are doomed to failure. This is the reason why Yahweh is made to say: "Come on! Let's go down and throw their language into confusion." However, the story may *originally* (before being recast) have had as its purpose to explain the differences in human language. Thus Chaine says: "The story is an answer of Hebrew folklore to the question of the origin of languages. The ancient Israelites thought that the diversity of tongues had brought about the diversity of peoples. We believe the contrary today. The slow formation of peoples brought about the slow formation of their languages. Already St. Gregory of Nyssa, a Father and Doctor of the Church, noted this. We must think in terms of many thousands of years when we consider that the Babylonian and Egyptian of the inscriptions have not appreciably varied during more than three thousand years! The story of languages is as old as that of mankind. It was not the Bible's purpose to offer information on these matters. It set forth the story of the Tower because the story contained religious teaching and perhaps, more than anything else, because it was one of those records that made it possible to tie up the story of Abraham with primitive events."[3]

Nor is it impossible that the Hebrew writers wished to include the story as a way of demeaning another enemy, the people of Babylon, seat of racial mingling and confusion. Here again we find the penchant for punning so characteristic of the Hebrews (and some moderns). Babel is made to derive from the Hebrew verb *balal*, to throw into confusion. This is not the real etymology. Babel derives from *bab-ili*, meaning *door of God.*

Gen 11, 10 brings us to another Priestly genealogy (11, 10–32) which will take us right up to Abraham. This genealogy is doubtlessly intended to parallel the P genealogy of chapter 5. Again we are given ten entries, and the formula is about the

[3] *Ibid.*, p. 167.

same, except that the writer does not bother to total the life-span of each patriarch, nor does he provide a formal death-notice. This he leaves to the reader. These patriarchs are all of the line of Shem. The Hebrew, Greek Septuagint, and Samaritan Pentateuch again present variant figures. A study of these numbers is most interesting and reveals their artificiality and "non-numerical" significance. Longevity was definitely on the decline, as we note by listing the totals from Shem down through Abraham: 600, 438, 433, 464, 239, 239, 230, 148, 205, and 175. And what is really curious, since the patriarchs father their sons at such an early age and live so long afterwards, there are really a mere 292 years from the Flood to Abraham, and Shem would have survived Abraham by 35 years! It was because the Septuagint translators noticed some of these peculiarities that they thought it better to juggle the figures—which they often did by adding an even 100 years to the date of fathering the first son. This widens the gap between the Flood and Abraham, attaining the length of 1,072 years —quite a difference!

What little we have said by no means exhausts the numerical puzzles of this genealogy. It does seem, however, that P was again interested in showing sin on the march, gradually reducing man's life-span to near-normal length; but he will raise it momentarily when a really good man comes along, such as Noah. The names in this genealogy partly overlap those given in the Table of Nations, 10, 21ff. It is of considerable interest that archaeology has found cities with the names of Serug and Nahor, and a tribe with the name of Reu. This brings us into the climate of chapter 10 once more, where peoples, cities, and individuals are curiously thrown together.

We have now been brought, through an elimination process (so common to the Old Testament), to the real beginning of Hebrew history—the call and life of Abraham, father of the Jewish people.

The editor of Genesis gave us what information he could assemble from an earlier age and is now ready to bring us into a different kind of writing, which we shall examine in the next chapter.

14   THE HEBREW PATRIARCHS: GENESIS 12—50

WHEN WE CROSS OVER from Gen 1—11 to 12—50 we come to a new literary form. It is best described as "Hebrew family history," stories about the great patriarchs of the Chosen People: Abraham, Isaac, Jacob, and Joseph. We note a strange silence regarding the really great world events of the time, those that would normally be regarded as important by historians. The specific name of the pharaoh who befriended Joseph is not even listed. This is obviously not history of an ordinary sort. It is rather a collection of accounts, often turning on births, marriages, and deaths, that would have had little interest to any save the Hebrew people themselves. These stories (no irreverence of any kind is intended) savor of the nomad campfire, where the anecdotes of tribe and people were recounted over and over by men who did little reading (for the obvious reason that scrolls were a rarity) but who had powerful memories that would put ours to shame. In fact, we could well refer to this section of Genesis as "what was remembered about the patriarchs." That the emphasis is on religion goes without saying —a sort of primitive catechetics—but we are still dealing with stories. Many of them are highly interesting; others are rep-

etitious (chapter 24 is a good example) or told in variant
forms (Gen 12, 10–20; 20, 1–18; 26, 1–11) and require no little
patience from the modern reader who is trained in getting to
the point.

The variant traditions, J, E, and P, are still at hand throughout this long section of Genesis, though at times it is not easy
to mark them off one from another. As these chapters are not
as important as the first eleven, we need not apprise our readers
of the precise tradition being used by the inspired editor in
any given place.

Let us make ourselves clear on one point. It was at one time
in vogue to question the very existence of the Hebrew patriarchs
and to look upon these stories as bereft of all historicity and
objectivity. While we may easily admit that a given tribesman
may actually stand for his tribe, the smashing critical attitudes
of the nineteenth century have been almost entirely abandoned
and our ideas on these chapters have been nicely readjusted.
This is largely due to the work of archaeological evidence. The
whole background of the patriarchal period has now been
wonderfully clarified, and we can see these Hebrew stalwarts
against an environment that shows how genuine the biblical
account is in many details. Thus the Nuzi marriage laws have
illustrated the marriage customs we encounter in the Jacob
cycle.[1] Ur of the Chaldees and Haran turn out to be allied,
both in trade and in religious devotion to the moon god, Sin.

Though the patriarchal sagas represent materials prefixed
to an already crystallized exodus-Sinai account, they are nonetheless basically reliable and throw much light on the primitive
phase of Hebrew history. Here the Jewish writers are no longer
borrowing and reworking the accounts of their neighbors; they
are recounting incidents that *belonged to them.*

Abraham is the father of the Jewish people (cf. Jn 8, 39).

[1] Cf. John Bright, *A History of Israel* (Philadelphia, Westminster, 1959),
p. 71.

He was called from a pagan, polytheistic region "beyond the river" (Jos 24, 1–3) to serve the One and Only God, Yahweh. That Abraham's monotheism left something to be desired is not only understandable; it is evident from a number of features throughout the patriarchal narratives. Some have referred to the Mosaic religion (including Abraham) as henotheism (acknowledging one god, while allowing that other people may acknowledge other, equally important, gods). So great a non-Catholic scholar as Harold H. Rowley is not content with this position, and asserts that "it can be established that [Moses] did not suppose that any other god but Yahweh counted."[2] Nonetheless, Abraham's monotheism was rudimentary, and the Genesis writers may well have projected something of their own developed monotheism back into their patriarchs. They, after all, had the benefit of the powerful monotheistic doctrine of the Second Isaiah (Is 40—55).

None of this jeopardizes the greatness of Abraham. He is rightly called "our patriarch" in the Canon of our Mass and is looked upon as a model of faith (see Rom 4, 1ff.; Hebr 11, 8ff.), for he heeded the instructions of God, though not understanding all that they entailed; he broke natural ties, set out for the unknown with his sterile wife, Sarah, and "hoped against hope" when he felt obliged to offer in sacrifice his only and long-awaited son, Isaac—his only avenue to the numerous progeny that God promised him.

On the other hand, it would not be correct to think of Abraham as one filled with the full ingredients of Christian perfection—a saint in the same sense as those who have been subjected to the gruelling process of canonization. That Abraham was willing to save himself at the expense of Sarah's virtue is hardly an indication of sanctity. For *those times*, nonetheless, he may be regarded as a fit instrument of God and a worthy founder of the Hebrew nation. Who can fail to admire

[2] *The Unity of the Bible* (Philadelphia, Westminster, 1955), p. 23.

him as he rushes out to offer hospitality to his mysterious guests
(Gen 18, 1ff.); as he lets his kinsman Lot have first choice of
the Palestinian grazing areas (Gen 13, 1ff.); as he trudges off
to sacrifice his only son Isaac in humble obedience to what he
thought was God's will (Gen 22, 1ff.); and as he sets out to
avenge the capture of Lot and, having succeeded, gives tithes
to Melkizedek, the mysterious priest-king of Jerusalem?

We notice throughout the patriarchal family stories the
process of selection or elimination about which we spoke earlier.
Thus Hagar's son Ishmael is not the recipient of the promises.
He, like Esau, is the founder of a tribe, but not allied to the
Chosen People.

Isaac, Abraham's long-awaited son, receives but scant attention in Genesis. He is simply dwarfed by his father and his
son. The suspicious attitude of Abraham towards the Canaanites
is shown by the fact that Isaac's wife, Rebecca, is sought out
from among relatives in Mesopotamia. Yet, and this is an interesting feature, Rebecca was hardly a monotheist. That she followed her husband, Isaac, in his religious belief is, however,
altogether likely. Ishmael and Esau have little scruple about
selecting their own wives. They are quite content with those
outside their family.

Rebecca's sterility (like Sarah's—a common biblical theme)
is amply atoned for by her twins. The constant jostling of these
twins within her womb caused her great anguish (enough to
drive her to some shrine for an explanation) and was meant to
signify the unhappy relations of the two peoples for which
they stood—Israelites and Edomites (Gen 25, 22-23).

As it turned out, Jacob and Esau (Israelites and Edomites)
never got along. Jacob stayed close to his mother, developed
astuteness and cleverness. Esau was the outdoor type, bluster-
ing but open. Jacob, at the behest of his mother, deceptively
obtained the blessing of the aged Isaac (Gen 27) after having
already obtained Esau's rights of primogeniture. Jacob is not

a man whom we easily admire, his slyness and craftiness leave the average reader cool; yet he is the heir of the promises. God's choices do not follow human standards.

Jacob's relations with Esau became so strained that he was advised to leave the country. He went to Mesopotamia, where he worked for Laban, at the same time seeking the hand of Rachel. Jacob was a clever herdsman and soon had Laban's flocks in the finest condition both as to quantity and as to breed. However, Laban's dishonesty with Jacob on his wedding night—passing off the weak-eyed and less desirable Leah in place of Rachel—marked a turning point in the relations of these two men. Though Jacob works another seven years for Rachel, he gets even with Laban by forming a further contract with him (asking only for the off-colored stock) which enriches Jacob at the expense of his father-in-law and necessitates another hasty departure. Jacob in Hebrew means "cheat." He is just that, and incurs rather regularly the displeasure of those around him. Yet his qualities were admired by the Hebrews and they enjoyed recounting his ability to make his way in the world. Rachel's lack of monotheism is indicated by her taking Laban's household gods before she leaves home. The act also had legal implications, indicating that she should ultimately receive her father's inheritance.

Jacob is famous as the father of twelve sons, founders of the twelve tribes of Israel. These sons are born of four women, Rachel and Leah and their two substitutes. The story of these births, beginning in Gen 29, 31, stands in decided contrast to a mentality that is only too widespread today: an unwillingness to bring children into the world, or at least unwillingness to accept all that result from normal marriage relations. Rachel and Leah can hardly wait for their next child: "Let me have children too," says Rachel, "or I shall die!"

To the name of each child is attached a popular etymology, as we might expect. Though Rachel herself has only two

children, Joseph and Benjamin, these are Jacob's favorite sons
(since Rachel was his favorite wife), and they always receive
special attention. We may note in the whole family life of
Jacob the bickering and jealousies that are the normal by-
product of bigamy or polygamy.

There are many incidents in the patriarchal stories that are
not easy to interpret. One such is the famous wrestling-match
recorded in 32, 23ff. The story has undoubtedly been recast at
least once, and for that reason it is difficult to put in its
original form. As it now stands, Jacob wrestles with no less
a person than God—and, what is more marvellous, he wins the
match! The story is meant to illustrate a number of points.
It explains the name of the town, Peniel; it serves as a favorable
presage to Jacob's dreaded meeting with his estranged brother
Esau; it accounts for his new name "Israel" (explained as meaning "he was strong against God"); Jacob also extracts a blessing
from God—no small thing in oriental eyes. To disengage the
historical kernel in such an account is next to impossible. While
this is very important to us today, it was not so for the sacred
writer. For him it was the lessons that counted, and it is these
lessons that we must seek out.

Jacob's sons are for the most part a none too virtuous lot.
Reuben defiles his father's marriage bed; Simeon and Levi
treacherously wipe out the male population of Shechem; Judah
is an adulterer and was proved to be just that by Thamar, his
daughter-in-law.

The shining light in the Jacob family is Joseph, and to him
the last section of Genesis (chapters 37 to 50) is dedicated. He
is sold into slavery by his own jealous brethren. Through dream-
interpreting abilities he rises to the highest offices in the Egyptian
court. His morals are shown to be beyond reproach as he spurns
the repeated propositions of Potiphar's wife. His foresight has
the entire Near East coming to Egypt begging and buying grain
as seven years of famine grip the oriental world. It was he who

saved the tiny Hebrew family (about seventy persons), bringing them to Egypt, arranging for their settlement in Goshen, setting them on the path to amazing increase. The stories that recount the unveiling of Joseph's identity to his guilty brethren are masterpieces of narrative; but they also illustrate the wonderful lessons of forgiveness and of divine providence bringing good out of evil.

Chapter 49 of Genesis is of special importance since it contains (*not* the Blessings, but) the Oracles of Jacob. These oracles, ostensibly forecasting the future of the various tribes, were doubtlessly "brought up to date" at a later period in Israelite history when the direction and tendencies of the various tribes were taking definite shape. The oracles have a distinct Canaanite background and stress particularly the importance of the strong tribe of Ephraim (one of Joseph's sons) and the even greater importance of the tribe of Judah, from which both David and Christ were to come. Gen 49, 10 is important and "messianic" (i.e. dealing with the *anointed king* of the line of David who will both lead and *deliver* his people): "The scepter shall not pass from Judah, nor the staff from between his feet, until he comes to whom it belongs; to him shall be the obedience of the peoples." Here we meet once more the selective process. Out of all the sons of Jacob, it is Judah who inherits the promises. It is he who prepares the way for Christ, "the lion of Judah" (Apoc 5, 5).

It is remarkable how these stories in Gen 12—50 were kept alive in the Hebrew memory over the long years that separated the time of their occurrence from their being put into writing. At the same time, practically nothing is recounted of the Egyptian sojourn which may have lasted as long as four hundred years. It is only towards its close that the book of Exodus mentions some incidents that led up to the Hebrew escape.

It would be a mistake to think of the patriarchal accounts of Genesis as being valueless. Many allusions are made to these stories in the New Testament. They figure into God's long-term plan of salvation—"salvation history." We have to admire the objectivity of the Hebrew narrators. They reveal to us the weaknesses as well as the greatness of their patriarchs. They do not conceal what is of little credit to their people. This lengthy section of the Bible has lessons that are of the highest value for us today: faith, trust, hospitality, generosity, chastity —all taught positively; plus many warning signs: "Don't do this!"

Our task, here as elsewhere, is to read the Bible intelligently, against its background, looking for its lessons and doctrine. As Catholics we believe that it is the Word of God, not dead or meaningless but a living and highly significant inspired message.

15 *MOSES AND THE EXODUS*

THE SECOND BOOK of the Bible is built almost entirely around *an event and a man*. The event is the exodus, including the trip to, and sojourn at, Mt. Sinai. The man is Moses: lawgiver, mediator, prophet, and deliverer of the Chosen People. The Sinai incident is one of the really great points in Old Testament theology and history. The book of Genesis was but a preparation for it; Sinai constitutes the kernel and starting-point of Old Testament writing; faithful Hebrews never allowed it to escape from their memories; the Prophets reminded them of it continually; the Jewish liturgical year, built around the Paschal feast (intimately connected with the exodus), reminded them of it; and the Psalms of the Hebrew people often featured the exodus-Sinai events: "When Israel went forth from Egypt, the house of Jacob from a people of foreign tongue, Judah became his sanctuary, Israel his domain. The sea saw it and fled; the Jordan turned back; the mountains skipped like rams, the hills like lambs" (Ps 114, 1–4). Above all, at Sinai the Hebrews became God's covenanted people and received through Moses from God their law as the standard of Covenant love and Covenant fidelity.

The book of Exodus enjoys a unique place in the Old Testament, and it is a key to much of the later Old and New Testament thought. The deliverance of the Jewish people from oppressive Egypt became a type of all divine interventions and deliverances. The return from the Babylonian captivity was conceived of by Second Isaiah as a new exodus. Even the redemptive work of Christ was thought of in terms of the exodus-event, for Christ's work was (and is) a deliverance, the formation of a new people, with a new and eternal covenant, with a new Law of love written on the hearts of the recipients of the Holy Spirit. This exodus goes on and on as we share more completely in the fruits of Redemption. Our Mass has a definite Paschal and therefore exodus setting. Endless are the valid parallels and types that we may discern in the book of Exodus foreshadowing Christian values.

Throughout the book of Exodus we will find the same Yahwist, Elohist, and Priestly traditions represented. The book is repetitious on some points, as a result; and later books of the Pentateuch, especially Leviticus and Deuteronomy, will also repeat a good deal of the matter that we are going to find here. The division between Genesis and Exodus is an artificial one, made at some time later than their final compilation.

Exodus is a Greek word, describing the main event of the book, just as Genesis is also Greek, describing the main event of that book. The Hebrews have never used these names, but have rather referred to the books by the words with which they begin. They call Exodus, *Weeleh Shemoth*, "And these are the names." The book grew into its final form with the passage of time, and many of its events are described here exactly as they came to be depicted and re-enacted at the great liturgical centers. Thus the events around Sinai, or the Crossing of the Reed Sea (the original text does not speak of the Red Sea), or the Plagues, are all the result of a liturgical recital meant to impress these events deeply upon the minds of the Hebrew worshippers. Such a presentation was aimed, as F. L. Moriarty, S.J., says, at "dynamic retention,"[1] for men are deeply impressed by a forceful portrayal and re-enactment of historical events.

The book of Exodus has two main parts: the Deliverance from Egypt (cc. 1, 1–15, 21) and the Covenant at Sinai (cc. 19, 1 to the end). Sandwiched in between these is a brief section (cc. 15, 22 to 18, 27) describing the Trek to Sinai.

As the book of Exodus opens, we find the Hebrews being terribly persecuted in Egypt. Long gone are the friendly conditions arranged by Joseph with the pharaoh of his time. Now the pharaoh is fearful of the rapidly increasing Hebrew population. Oppression causes the poorly organized people to cry out for mercy and deliverance. This is finally granted them through Moses, a man who had been spared in wondrous manner from the Egyptian persecutors, who had "been schooled in all the wisdom of the Egyptians" (Acts 7, 22); a man who knew desert life as a result of his stay with the Qenites in Midian; a man who had received a call from Yahweh to deliver his people.

After a long series of ten plagues, Moses finally leads the Hebrew people out of Egypt. The plagues are depicted as utterly devastating and brought on at the command of God's envoy. No single tradition contains them all, but the total is

[1] *Introducing the Old Testament* (Milwaukee, Bruce, 1960).

reached by gathering in the plagues from all three traditions. The most that any one tradition offers is seven. Egyptian annals have left no record of these plagues, and there is little doubt that the description of them in the Bible has been greatly hyperbolized in order to surround the exodus event with all the grandeur and marks of divine intervention that such a happening truly merits. The whole account is narrated in Exodus in a highly dramatic and epical form: the pharaoh again and again returns to his state of obduracy and stubbornness, even though any one of the plagues, as described, would have nearly crippled his kingdom. Such an account could hardly have failed to please the oriental reader. Surely he was impressed with the great significance of the exodus from Egypt.

The people that left Egypt are called Hebrews, a name that has probable affinities with a group of nomads known from other sources as the Hapiru—prominent in the thirteenth-twelfth centuries B.C., when the exodus took place. The Hebrews, however, gradually gained a monopoly on the term, and others of the class were forgotten. The group of people that left Egypt included "a crowd of mixed ancestry" (Exod 12, 38). Their number is set at 600,000 men (not including women and children) in Exod 12, 37—a number that is simply too high, for it would have entailed a total of some 2,000,000 departees. Some scholars think that the word "thousand" means "family" here, and this would surely ease the situation, but this solution is by no means certain. Everyone is agreed that so many people could not possibly have been led out of Egypt into the desert. The food problem alone would have been insurmountable, even allowing for whatever assistance the manna gave.

To read this book correctly we must never forget that its accounts were first stored up within the hearts of the Israelites. Only later were they written down. The book is an epic, and hence it tends to glorify, hyperbolize, and inflate the facts— numbers and events—rather constantly. While the events were historical, they were certainly not written up as we would write them up today. The modern reader can find plenty of evidence for this if he reads with open eyes.

The fact that there is still a manna tree on the Sinai peninsula which, through the work of insects, gives in limited quantity a substance (called "*mun*") almost exactly comparable in description to the biblical manna alerts us to the probable hyperbole of the manna accounts in the Old Testament—though this does not do away with some special intervention of God. The fact, too, that the book of Wisdom (16, 2ff.) went even further than Exodus and Numbers in its manna descriptions makes us consider the possibility that the Exodus account itself is exaggerated by the sacred writers, just as they have exaggerated the plague stories, the Crossing of the Reed Sea, the events at Sinai, and others.

This does not destroy the force or the meaning of the accounts in any way, but it does show us that the Hebrew writers wished to impress upon their readers the intervention of God in their history. This intervention (they felt, as did all other narrators of the ancient Near East) could be sufficiently shown only by the use of hyperbole—large numbers, stupendous events, and the omission of what we would today term secondary causes. The Bible nearly always makes God the direct agent of what happens—even to the point of having him "produce evil" in Is 45, 7 and "making Pharaoh obstinate" in Exod 10, 27. With all the evidence that has come to us from the ancient oriental literature, from the examination of the records, monuments, and the remains of the Near East, we can no longer read the book of Exodus as fundamentalists.

It would be a difficult task to write a scientific biography of Moses. There is no doubt that he existed; that the biblical stories centering on him are based on events that are fundamentally historical; that he was a great and heroic man; and that he gave the Hebrew people their Law and brought them into a

Covenant with Yahweh at Sinai. But our problems arise when we come to the details of his life—its length (e.g. the three forty-year periods that St. Stephen mentions in his speech recorded in Acts 7), his youth, the precise nature of his mystical experiences, the depth of monotheism that he professed. Readers who wish to see one of the fairest and most scientific treatments of this question could hardly do better than read the pages that touch on this question in Dr. John Bright's *A History of Israel.* Here every resource has been tapped, and the results are extremely satisfying. The Paulist Pamphlets[2] on *Exodus,* written by Father Roland E. Murphy, O.Carm., in 1960, are likewise of the greatest value, even though they are popularizations and cannot always give the complete reasons for the conclusions drawn and set before the public.

We have mentioned that the Hebrew text of Exodus never uses the term "Red" Sea. It speaks of "Yam Suph," and that means "Sea of Reeds" (the Red Sea has no reeds). This again is important in getting at the objective facts of the Crossing of the Sea as the Israelites escaped from the Egyptians. Those who saw the film "The Ten Commandments" will recall the majestic depiction of this crossing, and most portrayals are comparable to it. Here again, the scholar feels obliged to speak of hyperbole—to bring up the fact that a fleeing people would hardly head for the deepest waters to make its crossing, even though it had the greatest trust in God's omnipotence. The Hebrew people almost certainly crossed the Reed Sea, a marshy area about midway in the present-day Suez Canal, where the water was perhaps waist-high. The entire story, of course, is told on a grandiose scale, but this is exactly what we should expect, for the event was important, and the narrators had a perfect right to embellish it in the telling. Just look again at the psalm verse that we cited near the beginning of this chapter

[2] New York, Paulist Press.

where the mountains and hills skip like lambs and the waters turn back.

After a three months journey, the Israelites arrived at Mt. Sinai. The identification of this peak has always been a problem, for the Bible does not describe its locality in anything like a specific manner. There is, nonetheless, an ancient and worthy tradition that the mountain now called Jebel Mousa (Mt. Moses), rather far south on the Sinai peninsula, is the mountain which the Bible refers to as Sinai (or Horeb). Most visitors to Sinai are sufficiently impressed with its appearance, surroundings, and height (7,497 ft.) to allow at least for the possibility that it is the Mt. Sinai of the Bible. To be assertive on the matter is another question altogether.

In any case, the events at Sinai, though mysterious, are of the highest significance in Israelite history. Here a rugged and heterogeneous people entered in a Covenant with Yahweh and receive a Law, Moses serving as mediator between themselves and God. However, we may as well be frank; it is again difficult to settle on many details. How much of the Law, for example, was directly revealed to Moses? The question is not an idle one, especially when other ancient legal systems which have been discovered have shown remarkable similarities to points within the Hebrew Law. To assert complete independence of the Mosaic Law from these systems, e.g. the Code of Hammurabi, would be foolhardy and would betray ignorance of the facts at issue. On the other hand, the Mosaic Law is often (though not always) superior and clearer on many points. Again, we are at a loss to sift from the biblical story the exact amount of cold fact, and especially to define the nature of Moses' experiences on the holy mount. As with other mystical experiences, e.g. those of St. Teresa of Avila, an evaluation (even by the mystic) is very difficult.

We are also somewhat at a loss to state whether or not Moses was the first in history to know Yahweh. The accounts in Exod 3 and 6 differ on the point and render a final decision nearly impossible. The same indefiniteness remains with us when we ask how thoroughly monotheistic Moses' outlook was. I would not hesitate to call Moses a monotheist, but I would feel forced to qualify this with some term such as "initial," "germinal" or "imperfect." This, as we have seen, is the position taken by Professor Harold Rowley.[3] The whole question has been profoundly studied by Dr. W. F. Albright in his book *From the Stone Age to Christianity: Monotheism and the Historical Process.*[4]

The book of Exodus offers many details of Hebrew Law and liturgical regulations. It also describes in minute detail—sometimes twice over—the construction of the Tabernacle, altars, and other cultic objects, and also the organization of the Hebrew priesthood, etc. Much of this material stems from a later age and was merely projected back into the framework of the life of Moses—for he was *the* Hebrew lawgiver. The material is nonetheless of the greatest value, no matter what its age-length may be.

Despite these and many other genuine problems that we encounter as we go through Exodus, it is one of the most significant books of the entire Bible. All that it contains is built around that event which the Hebrews considered to be the greatest (the exodus from Egypt and the happenings at Sinai) and around that man like to whom no other ever arose in pre-Christian Israel, Moses (Dt. 34, 10).

[3] *Op. cit.*, p. 23.
[4] Garden City, New York, Doubleday Anchor Books, 2nd ed., 1957.

16 *JOSHUA, THE CONQUEST, AND THE JUDGES*

THE HEBREW BIBLE contains three collections of books: the Law (including Genesis, Exodus, Leviticus, Numbers, and Deuteronomy); the *Prophets;* and the *Writings.* Opening the second collection is the book of Joshua. Though Christian scholars have often placed Joshua among the "historical books," there is much wisdom in the ancient Hebrew classification. Joshua, like the Prophets, *has a message for us from God*—and this is the very essence of Hebrew prophecy. The Prophets spoke in the name of God, and their words could refer to past, present, or future. Father Luke Grollenberg, O.P., in his famous *Atlas of the Bible* offers this additional explanation: "The Jews classified Joshua and Judges among the prophetic writings. This means that their compilers assembled and worked over the documents with the idea of using this presentation of memorable events in the history of Israel as a vehicle for preaching the faith."[1]

The book of Joshua is an epic. Though historical, it is written according to very different standards from those of present-day history. All the records and memories of the conquest and partitioning of the land of Canaan were compiled together, even though many of the accounts had been greatly hyperbolized and dramatically heightened in the narration. The book glows with enthusiasm as it recounts the rapid strategic victories of the Israelite army and the division of the land among the tribes.

[1] New York and London, Nelson, 1956–7, p. 56.

This was no ordinary moment in Hebrew history. For the acquisition of their own land the Hebrews had waited a long time. The great patriarchs, Abraham, Isaac, and Jacob had only sojourned in Palestine; they were not landowners. Abraham had acquired limited burial rights at Makpelah, near Hebron, but that was all. At last the land was falling to the Chosen People! It was to become the Holy Land, and every inch of it was precious in Hebrew eyes, even as it is to the modern State of Israel, though under greatly changed conditions. If the book dwells inordinately (for the modern reader) on geographical details, we should recall how dear this land was to its Hebrew occupants.

The book centers on the hero, Joshua. He had long been singled out as the successor of Moses, and was a man tried and approved. One tradition makes him already a great warrior before the arrival at Sinai (Exod 17, 8–14); more often he is presented as one of Moses' most trusted companions, going up the holy mount with the legislator (Exod 24, 13). His name had once been Hoshea, but it was changed (according to Num 13, 16) to Joshua, i.e. "Yahweh saves."

Joshua was an outstanding person—a man of God, a courageous warrior and clever strategist, relentless in carrying out what was seen as God's will, even though some of his work will strike us as brutal and cruel. The lavish praise of Ben Sirah (46, 1–8) is added proof of the reputation that he enjoyed in Jewish annals.

The book of Joshua is a deeply religious epic. It presents the entire conquest as a holy war: the Canaanites, with all their pagan worship, are to be exterminated, and the land, as the abode of a theocratic people, is to become dedicated to God. The theme of the book might easily be stated in a phrase that occurs several times: ". . . Yahweh was fighting for his people" 10, 14). It was the religious lessons of the book that the Hebrew people were to grasp as its contents were recited.

There are countless interesting incidents in Joshua, and we can only treat them lightly here. Chapter 1 sets the tone for the entire book (reading much like Deuteronomy) and offers distinct edification. The second chapter, however, will prove a little disconcerting as Joshua's spies, sent from across the Jordan to look over the city of Jericho, the first object of attack, find themselves in the house of Rahab, a harlot. Without attempting to exculpate the spies entirely, we should bear in mind that inns served several purposes. If there was any place where information could be picked up, it was there. Rahab, whatever her failures may have been, gains for herself eternal renown because of her "faith" (Heb 11, 31) and her "works" (Jas 2, 25) by aiding the Hebrew spies and asking them to protect her home and family in the coming attack.

With the Crossing of the Jordan in chapters 3—4 (described in terms very similar to the account of the Reed Sea Crossing) we enter on a series of stupendous happenings. The story, really told twice, according to two variant traditions, has no doubt been built up, and it is impossible to pare away the hyperbole from the cold facts. To seek explanations of the event in cave-ins of the Jordan's banks, such as actually took place in 1267 and again as late as 1927, hardly seems to be the right approach. In nearly all the miraculous events recorded in Joshua, we will more likely be faithful to the intention of the biblical writer if we simply point out that the events were recorded as they had come to be described beforehand in oral and written tradition, and that the precise historical nature of the events was not the chief concern. On the one hand there is some kind of divine intervention; on the other there is nearly always hyperbole. To be more precise than this is usually no more than guesswork on our part.

The Hebrews established a base camp at Gilgal. From here they worked out. Jericho, as we have said, was the first object of attack. The story of its fall is undoubtedly hyperbolized, and the idea of the gigantic crumbling walls is prevalent as a result of numerous pictures and descriptions. That the Hebrews took the city is something we need not call into doubt. That they took it in the manner described in Jos 6, 1–25 is highly unlikely. The words "and the walls fell down flat" (Knox) need mean no more than that the city fell to the Hebrews. For an interesting discussion of this, see the fine little volume by Father Alexander Jones, *Unless Some Man Show Me*.[2] Excavation work carried on in recent years at Jericho by Miss Kathleen Kenyon has negatived earlier enthusiastic reports, especially those by John Garstang—at one time accepted by so great an archaeologist as the late L. H. Vincent, O.P. (reported in the *Catholic Commentary on Holy Scripture*).[3] Today, it has been conclusively shown that Jericho mound (Tell es-Sultân) yields no information of any kind on the Joshuan Era. There is a strange blank in the strata of that period, even allowing for any possible latitudes in time (1500 to 1200 B.C.). Thus archaeology neither confirms nor absolutely disproves the biblical information on Jericho. Rather it puts us on guard against accepting the story too much at face value.

Ai ("ruins") and Bethel both fell to Joshua, though not without a stern lesson in obedience (at Achan's expense). Ai presents another archaeological enigma, for the site seems to have been unoccupied from around 2400 to 1000 B.C., and hence would not have been inhabited during Joshua's lifetime. No satisfactory solution for this problem has ever been worked out, though a number of suggestions have been tendered, such as a confusion of names in the sacred text (W. F. Albright), Bethel's destruction having been transferred in oral tradition to the nearby "ruins" to explain its condition.

The ruse of the Gibeonites brings us into one of the most famous of all biblical questions—one implicated in the Galileo

[2] New York, Sheed & Ward, 1951, pp. 26–8.

[3] New York and London, Nelson, 1956–7, p. 283.

case. When the Gibeonites had deceitfully won Israelite alle-
giance and were being attacked by a coalition army gathered by
five Amorite petty kings they signalled to Joshua for help. He
brought his army to Gibeon and fought a famous battle in
which he massacred the coalition army that had been raised to
punish the Gibeonites. It is in connection with this fray that
the famous "sun stoppage" incident is recorded. Examine the
text (Jos 10, 7-15) for yourself to see how it reads. It is
referred to again in Ben Sirah 46, 4 (or 5). Scholars have
thought up all kinds of explanations for this event (the writer
once listed some twenty of them in his class notes), for it is
no small matter for the sun actually to stop in its course for
twenty-four hours while a battle is being fought, even if it
were the greatest of battles—which this wasn't.

The remarks of Joseph J. de Vault, S.J., in the *Paulist Pamphlet
Bible Series,* give a fairly good picture of present-day scholarly
opinion on the subject: "Joshua 10, 7-15 has caused no little
trouble to readers in the past, particularly verses 12-15, the
'sun-miracle.' In explanation of the text, we should remark first
of all, that we have here two views of the battle. The first is
in prose (vv. 7-11) and records the fact of the great victory
achieved with Yahweh's help in the form of a mighty hailstorm.
The second is poetic (vv. 12-14) and gives Joshua's famous
war-cry apostrophizing the sun and the moon. This is followed
by an editor's comment. Attempts have been made even in
modern times to explain the sun's 'standing still' on the basis
of a prolonged daylight due to refraction of light, or as a
meteor shower or some other such phenomenon. These pseudo-
scientific 'explanations' collapse of their own tortured weight.
Happily, they are being replaced by a sane exegesis which
recognizes the passage for what it is—a highly poetical version
of an emotionally charged cry of Joshua, who hoped for
time, for daylight, in which to crush the enemy utterly. The
enemy was crushed, so the time was granted, and this was

expressed poetically in verse 13a, prosaically in verse 13b."[4] Ben
Sirah does no more than repeat the statements that were found
in these verses.

Excavations at the various sites conquered by Joshua (Lakish,
Eglon, Debir, Hazor, etc.) have led to the conclusion that his
blitz compaign was carried out in the thirteenth century B.C.
(i.e. the 1200's). Though certain passages in the book (e.g. 10,
40–43; 11, 23) would lead us to believe that Joshua's victory
was complete and overwhelming, other sections (e.g. 13, 1–6)
show that this was not what happened. Much of Palestine was
left to be conquered. Jerusalem, for example, was never taken
until about the year 1000 B.C. during the reign of David (approximately 1010–970 B.C.), even though Jdg 1, 8 presents an
anticipatory gloss that is shown up by 1, 21.

The book of Judges tells the post-Joshua story. It was not
easy for the Israelites, never well-organized, to hold their con-
quests in Canaan. They were constantly harassed by Canaanites
and outsiders. These attacks are attributed by the writer of
Judges to the repeated infidelities of the Jewish people. Yahweh
punished his people by allowing the enemy to dominate them
temporarily. The Judges are primarily *inspired military leaders*
raised up by God to deliver the people from their plight. Many
of them must have lived simultaneously, and we are obliged by
chronological certainties to situate them all between 1200 and
1050 B.C. To think of the Judges as legal experts is quite inexact.
There is scant evidence that they operated in this way, Deborah
(Jdg·4, 4–6) being a partial exception.

Few of the Judges are men whom we could describe as saints.
Gideon, though assuredly zealous for the welfare of his people
and to some extent for the triumph of Yahwism over Baalism,
would hardly qualify for canonization. His extreme vengeance
upon Succoth's chieftains (8, 13) and his idolatry (8, 27) bring
out his rough edges.

[4] P. 20.

Jephthah, as good a warrior as he was, acted imprudently and rashly in vowing the life of the first one who would come to meet him as he returned from battle (11, 29–40) and he had no right to carry out his vow at the expense of his innocent daughter.

Samson is well described by J. L. McKenzie, S.J., in *The Two-Edged Sword* as "a brutal, wenching lout with astonishing strength."[5] This "judge" is something of a one-man army, yet he seems to qualify less than all the others for the title. The stories that grew up around him have a little of the Paul Bunyan about them. Above all, the term "saint" hardly fits this figure, as colorful as he may otherwise be. There is no reason why we should strain ourselves to make saints of all the biblical (especially Old Testament) characters, when the Bible itself does not attempt this. It is quite realistic about the entire matter and presents some of the finest and most objective character studies that one could find anywhere.

The books of Joshua and Judges, while having some great and essential religious lessons, present the rougher and harsher side of Hebrew life. They prepare us for the coming monarchy. The editorial comment Jdg 17, 6; 18, 1; 19, 1; and 21, 25 speaks volumes: "At that time there was no king in Israel, and each one did as he pleased."

The system of "herem" (total-destruction) warfare is attributed to a direct command of Yahweh. There were, of course, serious reasons for such warfare, and it was common at the time. Yahwism would have plenty of trouble surviving without the added temptations of the idolatrous and licentious Canaanites living in and around the still wavering Hebrew monotheists. It does seem, nonetheless, that such warfare was merely *interpreted* and phrased as the will of Yahweh. Somewhat similarly, Abraham *thought* that Yahweh wished him to take the life of his only son, Isaac; this, too, was expressed as a command from Yahweh. This is not an uncommon biblical process. The Hebrews them-

[5] P. 135.

selves would not have seen any moral problem in extermination warfare.

We will have a hard time ever understanding the Old Testament if we demand of it a Christian morality and ideal—one which we ourselves, as is only too evident, frequently fail to acquire. How many Christian armies have not committed atrocities that would make those of the Hebrew occupation force look insignificant? When all is said and done, we must admire the wonderful objectivity of the Old Testament writers, especially in describing their own moral deficiencies, nor should we fail to consider that Hebrew standards were generally much higher than those of their contemporaries.

17 *THE HEBREW MONARCHY*

THE PERIOD OF THE JUDGES (1200–1050) was, as we have seen, a time of violence and internal disorder. Such a condition became all the more serious as the friction between Israel and her enemies, especially the Philistines, mounted. Obstacles to the conquest and retention of the Promised land were plentiful enough without this added difficulty. Dr. W. F. Albright has stated in *The Biblical Period:* "An impartial observer of the early twelfth century B.C. would probably have said that everything was against the success of the Israelite experiment."[1] And he goes on to explain (in a remarkable little volume, which he, nonetheless, now regards as slightly dated) all the factors that stood in the way of full conquest: Israelite cultural backward-

[1] Pittsburgh, 1950, p. 17.

ness; ignorance of Canaanite combat methods; broken Canaanite
terrain rendering communications difficult; the iron monopoly of
the Philistines; and the constant tendency within Israel toward
selfishness and tribal separatism. Had it not been for the weakness of Egypt at that time, the conquest, humanly speaking,
would have been ruled out.

More than the Canaanite opposition, however, was the growing power of the Philistine invaders who entered Palestine (and
to which they were eventually, by a strange irony of history,
to give their name) from the Mediterranean isles from the west
about the same time as the Israelites swept in from the east.
Samson had coped with the Philistines, but ineffectually. Their
incursions were getting beyond all control.

In the meantime, a man named Samuel had gained ascendancy
among the Hebrews. All Scripture readers have enjoyed the
marvellous stories that surround his birth from the sterile
Hannah, his admirable fidelity during the times of the lax
priest Eli and his two worthless sons Hophni and Phinehas,
and his fame that daily grew from Dan to Beersheba. Gradually
Samuel became the spiritual giant among the Israelites, famed
for his holiness and wisdom. Upon the death of Eli, he took
over the leadership. He was not merely high-priest, but also
the last of the Judges and a prophet. As far as we know, he
was not much of a military leader, but he did know how to
direct warfare from a distance, and especially how to tackle the
knottiest problems of conscience and to set policies. Samuel, as
we are interestingly informed in 1 Sm 9, 9, was known as a
"seer"—an older name for "prophet." Samuel was content with
the status quo and planned to pass his office on to his sons,
Joel and Abijah. They attempted to function at Beersheba for
a time, but they were so unlike their father, "taking bribes and
perverting justice" (cf. 1 Sm 8, 1ff.), that this plan was
obviously destined to failure.

In the meantime the Israelites began to demand a king—

the only way to defeat the Philistines. Other nations had strong central authority. Why should they not have a king? Reactions to this demand were decidedly mixed. Samuel himself showed the greatest displeasure at the idea (1 Sm 8, 6ff.). God was their king. To set up an earthly king would be effrontery.

There had been an effort at kingship already. Abimelek, son of Gideon, had tried to make himself king, but was finally slain by—of all things—a woman as he attacked Thebez (cf. Jdg 9, 53ff.). Deuteronomy (17, 14-20) speaks of the evils of a future kingship, but this is really a literary fiction, for the book was written some centuries after the inception of the monarchy and the author knew only too well *from experience* the disadvantages of monarchy.

When the opposition to the old regime became too vociferous, Samuel yielded and Saul became Israel's first king. He was kept under Samuel's thumb, though he was himself a striking and capable man. Saul was a popular hero, a warrior, a man of gigantic build, yet depicted as somewhat timid (1 Sm 10, 22). Deep down in his nature lurked a spirit of jealousy and tyranny, and these were the qualities that would gradually ruin him. Saul does not receive a long, exclusive treatment in 1 Samuel. As a matter of fact, after a few imposing victories, his disobedience to Samuel (and hence to God) become pronounced—first at Gilgal, and then in sparing the Amalekites. Soon Saul breaks with Samuel, the latter announcing his rejection in the strongest terms: "To obey is better than sacrifice, to hearken is superior to the fat of rams. Because you have rejected the word of the Lord, he has rejected you from being king."

Saul then became jealous of David, an outstanding young warrior. He soon broke with David—though he realized his goodness, one so filled with respect for God's anointed king. Saul finally went to the extreme of slaying the family of Eli at Nob because they had befriended David as he went into flight. This, according to Dr. Albright, marked Saul's definitive abandonment of official Yahwism and the accentuation of a demented condition that would plague Saul to his bitter end when he fell before the Philistines on the mountains of Gilboa. Saul's is a tragic case. His huge, trembling frame prostrate on the floor of the medium's dwelling at Endor offers a lesson that we can ill afford to let slip by. His rejection was the result of pride, with its companions, jealousy and disobedience.

Excavations at Gibeah have shown that Saul lived a very unpretentious life, for the kingship was as yet without traditions and customs. In this we can only admire Saul and understand something of his plight. He didn't quite know how to conduct himself as king; yet he could have listened to Samuel and he could have been a highly successful ruler, but he did neither the one nor the other. He reigned from around 1020 to 1000 B.C.

The books of Samuel give most of their space to David, and deservedly so. The stories that concern him encroach heavily on those concerning Saul. David is a tremendously important figure, though far from the perfection that we associate with Christian sanctity. He was so popular that there were several stories as to how he rose to fame. The Goliath story is one—a story, by the way, that quite possibly did not belong to David, for 2 Sm 21, 19 attributes the victory over Goliath to one Elhanan, son of Jaareoregim, the Bethlehemite. Another story has him coming into fame through his musical talent: his ability to soothe the troubled spirits of the tortured Saul.

In whatever way he may actually have come to public notice, David was deeply loved by the Hebrews, and on many scores. Warrior, strategist, administrator, general, on occasion an outlaw, he was at the same time a man of charm, a musician, deeply religious, an inspired composer of psalms. It was David who expanded the boundaries of Israel as they had never been expanded previously; it was David who beat back the Philistines so that they were never more a serious threat; it was David who prepared for the peaceful reign of Solomon; it was David who by "sheer political genius" (W. F. Albright) captured the Jebusite city of Jerusalem and made it his capital, thus giving his state not only a nearly impregnable fortress but also a centrally located, non-partisan site for his city—the city of David, or Zion. It was David who brought the Ark of the Covenant to Jerusalem, thus making the city a religious center of the tribal kingdom, one that gradually absorbed the attention given other shrines; and it was David who took a deep interest in sacred worship, composing not a few of the Psalms. Finally, it was David to whom Nathan (2 Sm 7, 11–16) addressed the famous dynastic oracle, promising the Davidic line perpetuity and the special attentions of divine providence. Thus "Messianism" (the hope that centered around the "Meshiah," the anointed Davidic king) was born, and it was from the Davidic line that our Divine Saviour came. These are but some of David's claims to our admiration. Had we the outlook of the Chronicler (who tended to omit the ignoble deeds of David), we would perhaps stop here; but, with the writer of Samuel, we must be honest enough to point out David's less admirable side.

In David's life there was a continual upsurge until his unfortunate relationship with Bathsheba, wife of the lowly but loyal Hittite soldier, Uriah. From that time on, David's life becomes horribly entangled and clouded. One difficulty after another arises. David had been such a rough and cruel warrior that Nathan had to tell him that he was no man to build a temple for Yahweh; but now one sin led to another: adultery, murder, domestic troubles, his sons angling for his throne, and rebellion.

David's final instructions to Solomon are far from edifying. One after another, different trouble-makers are to be put out of the way, even men to whom David had promised clemency, such as Shimei. Joab, who had been as loyal to David as he was unscrupulous towards others, would also have to go. Israel's second king, whose rule extended over approximately forty years (around 1000 to 961 B.C.), is no less a subject for extended meditation than Saul.

Strangely enough, the Israelites seem to have passed over the blemishes in David's character. He remained fixed in their minds as a great king, and they did not hesitate to think of a new David arising—the Messiah—one who would surpass David, yet have the marks of this king who loved God so vehemently, despite his sins.

The whole Psalter, as we hope to show later on, would come to be attributed to this king who only wrote some of the psalms, but who became, like Moses with respect to the Pentateuch or Solomon to the Wisdom literature, a kind of patron-writer of *all* these sacred songs.

David's successor on the Israelite throne was Solomon, whose name in Hebrew (Shelomo) is almost equal to the word for peace (*shalom*). Solomon marks the zenith of Israelite international prestige and material prosperity. He established commerce, industry (archaeology has discovered his copper mines and smelters in the area south of the Dead Sea, as well as his stables at Megiddo), and lavish court life. That Solomon had three hundred wives and seven hundred consorts is strong hyperbole, but harems were a part of royal display and a sign of international acceptance, where marriages often sealed good foreign relations.

The only trouble was that these foreign wives brought along their own religions and gods and weren't bashful about demanding decent sanctuaries for them right in Jerusalem. It took money to live this kind of life and it came in large part from bleeding the people with heavy tax burdens. Solomon was noted for wisdom, and the Queen of Sheba, who came to arrange for trade relations, was aghast at what she saw and heard. Solomon had the great honor of constructing the first temple in Jerusalem—which, however, was not as grandiose as his own royal palace (cf. 1 Kgs cc. 5—8).

It is not without reason that his whole reign has been compared to that of Louis XIV of France. It was a giant bubble that was destined to burst, and the thorough disgust of the ordinary people with Solomon is clearly shown by the scene that takes place after his death. The northern tribes meet with Rehoboam and demand better treatment, under threat of secession. Rehoboam's foolish answer to their demands (be sure to read 1 Kgs 12, 1ff.) is responsible for the tragic split of Israel into two kingdoms: the ten tribes of the north, called Israel, with its capital at various sites, but especially at Samaria; the two tribes of the south, called Judah, with its capital at Jerusalem, under the leadership of Rehoboam and the Davidic line. It was a sorry moment in Israelite history and would lead to deplorable results. This split took place somewhere around 931 B.C. The northern kingdom, which established its own counter-shrines at Bethel and Dan, lasted about two hundred years. It was wrecked by the Assyrian monarch Sargon II, who took Samaria and led many of the northerners captive. The southern kingdom lasted all the way down to 586, when it fell to Nebuchadnezzar, the neo-Babylonian monarch, who likewise deported many of the southerners.

The kings of Israel failed as a group because they did not subject their rules to the will of Yahweh. They strove in too many cases to vie with the pagan monarchs around them. It is a sad fact that the really good kings were extremely few. The sacred writers (who favored the southern kingdom) cannot list a single good king in the north, where murder commonly ended one dynasty and began a new one. They scrape and dredge, and they can only present us with two really good kings in the south. These are Hezekiah (the famous tunnel-builder, through whose fabulous 1,777-foot watercourse Jerusalem visitors may slosh their way even today—an experience never to be forgotten) and Josiah. It is this latter who really deserves the palm. While 2

Kgs 20, 19 brings out the selfishness (preceded by imprudence) of Hezekiah, with Josiah we can find little fault.

One of the messianic psalms (89), at times a nearly verbatim citation of the Nathan-oracle (2 Sm 7), shows the disappointment of the Israelites with their kings prior to, or perhaps just after, the fall of Jerusalem—when the monarchy came to an end. "You have renounced the covenant with your servant; you have defiled his crown in the dust. . . . How long, O Lord? Will you hide yourself for ever? . . . Lord, where is your steadfast love of old, which by your faithfulness you swore to David?" (vv. 39, 46, 49).

The monarchy came to an ignominious close. But the last word had not been spoken. There was still the oracle of Nathan, and the Hebrews did not forget it. They had faith enough to hope for a new David. *And he came,* in the form of God-and-man, united in One Divine Person, "descended from David according to the flesh" (Rom 1, 3). God does not fail to keep his word.

During the monarchy—and even before it, to some extent—there was another Israelite institution that gained great momentum and served as the conscience of the nation where king and priest had failed. We are speaking of the prophets. They are too big to be lumped together with anyone else—and they are really too big for just one chapter in a book.

"THEN THE LORD stretched forth his hand and touched my mouth. And the Lord said to me: Behold! *I am putting my words in your mouth;* behold, this day I am giving you authority over the nations and kingdoms, to root up and to pull down, to wreck and to ruin, to build and to plant" (Jer 1, 9–10).

The Jewish kingdom was never very significant when compared with the other kingdoms around her: Egypt, Assyria, Syria, Babylonia, Persia, Greece, or Rome. However, despite internal weaknesses and backsliding, despite unworthy kings and priests, she had one spontaneous institution that continually sparked her to life as long as it lasted. This was prophetism.

No other nation has ever produced a phenomenon like to that of the true prophets of Israel—men of the highest ideals, not usually popular with state officials, sometimes counterfeited by cheap imitations and impostors, but, when authentic, real activators of the national conscience. We hear of them nearly all the way through the Bible, in one form or another, but their Golden Age seems to have lasted not much over five hundred years, 900 to 400 B.C. serving as wide termini.

There are many erroneous notions about biblical prophets lurking in the average mind; so before attempting anything like a definition it might be profitable for us to have a look at the prophets in the Bible and then see if we can't find some common denominator for all.

Already in Gen 20, 7 Abraham is called a prophet. The king of Gerar was informed of this, as the account states it, by the Lord in a dream. (We should remember that many biblical accounts, such as this, were composed centuries after the time of the events described.) Abraham was, as we have seen, a man who seems to have had many communications from God—in whatever form they came to him.

Moses, too, in Dt 34, 10, is called a prophet—even the greatest of the prophets, "with whom the Lord held converse face to face." We also meet schools of ecstatic prophets, men who went about singing, exciting themselves, dancing, making incoherent utterances, whose activities seemed contagious enough to draw others into their midst (cf. 1 Sm 10, 9ff.; see also Num 11, 24ff.). This type of prophet is mysterious, nor does he capture our admiration in every way. Other groups of prophets, such as those that gathered around Elijah and Elisha, conduct themselves a little more sensibly (cf. 2 Kgs 2, 3ff.). Some of the prophets never seem to have written anything themselves, e.g. Elijah, while others seem to have both spoken and written—though the oral work was always uppermost in their vocation. Where writings are found, they were often set down by others, not the prophets themselves, who seem to have had their hands full just delivering the messages they received.

The prophets were called from every form of life: farming (Amos); statesmanship (Isaiah); priesthood (Ezekiel); kingship (David). Jeremiah was a celibate, Hosea married, etc. There is no limitation on the call of God—even today.

Some of the prophets strike us as highly sensible men (Nathan), while most of them not only impress *us* as being odd, but their contemporaries seem to have found them that way too. The noble Isaiah walked about Jerusalem with a yoke around his neck, but otherwise naked (Is 20, 3–4); Ezekiel was noted for the most unusual antic-prophecies by which he aroused the curiosity of his fellow-captives at Tel-Abib (though he attains rare literary heights, too); Jeremiah rarely had a good word for the leaders of the southern kingdom and was looked upon as a fanatic and nuisance; Amos was unpolitely told to leave the precincts of the northern kingdom (Amos 7, 12–13); Elijah, as powerful a figure as he was, went about clothed in an unusual manner, and must have made himself most annoying by his continuous and fearless denunciations of people and policies, not to speak of his odd manners.

Yet, it is just this that we have to admire: as odd as these men may have been, they had the deepest conviction of being God's mouthpieces, and they announced the message of God with a fearlessness and single-mindedness that would put most of us to shame—and which put their contemporaries to shame. Some of the prophets answered their call willingly (Isaiah was anxious to be sent, Is 6, 8); and still others were exhausted by their communications from God (Dan 8, 27); and still others never tired of complaining that it was no easy task to function as a prophet (Jer 20, 7ff.). Some of the prophets were educated and spoke in magnificent cadenced phrases (Isaiah), others were but little schooled and had to use the simple language of the rustics (Amos). Some were verbose (Jeremiah is the longest of all the prophetic books), others have left us hardly anything at all (Obadiah)—though we can only make an insecure judgment since the amount of written material would not necessarily indicate the amount of spoken material.

The prophets talk about the past, the present, and the future —but not all of them about all three. Some feature the present, others the future, but most of them mingle all three perspectives. If they speak about the future it is generally vague, with heavy reference to what is happening or to what has happened. Thus when Micah seems to foretell the birth of Christ from Bethlehem (5, 2), it is probably no more than a reference to the fact that David—the first of the messianic line—was born there, and that if the great Messiah to come is anything like David he will also be born in Bethlehem.

There has always been a tendency to reduce the prophets to

men peering into the future with the clearest vision and describing for us in minute detail, centuries in advance, what is going to take place. This, however, is rarely the case, and a good deal of our apologetics based on this kind of assumption will not stand the sincere and unprejudiced tests of scholarly scrutiny. Almost all recent research, e.g. the famous Journées Bibliques of Louvain in 1952, with the resulting volume, *L'Attente du Messie*,[1] has shown the weaknesses of such a system.

At all events, the real mark of a prophet, the common denominator that all of them share, is that the prophet receives and utters the authentic word of God—whether it refers to past, present, or future, no matter for or against whom it happens to be. False prophets there surely were (cf. 1 Kgs 22, 1-28, where Micaiah son of Imlah is pitted against Zedekiah and some four hundred false prophets); weak prophets there were, too (cf. 1 Kgs 13, 8ff.), but what distinguishes a true prophet, called by God (hence not merely an ecstatic), is his conviction of possessing and having to deliver the message of God. ". . . day in, day out, nothing it earns me, this divine spokesmanship, but reproach and mockery. Did I essay to put the Lord out of my thoughts, and speak no more in his name, all at once it seemed as though a raging fire were locked in my bosom, pierced my whole frame, till I was worn out with it, and could bear no more" (Jer 20, 8-9, Knox). The prophet was God's mouthpiece: "When the lion roars who does not fear? When the Lord God speaks, who will not prophesy?" (Amos 3, 8). Our English word "prophet" comes from the Greek *prophētēs*, meaning "one who speaks on behalf of." The customary Hebrew word for prophet is *nabi'*, the etymology of which is doubtful. It may mean "one called" or "one who is inspired by God"—nor does this exhaust the possibilities.

The prophets make up the largest section of the Hebrew Bible, as we have seen, and include Joshua, Judges, Samuel and Kings

[1] Bruges, Desclée de Brouwer, 1954.

(Early Prophets); and Isaiah, Jeremiah, Ezekiel, Hosea, Amos, Joel, Obadiah, Jonah, Micah, Nahum, Habakkuk, Zephaniah, Haggai, Zechariah, and Malachi (Later Prophets—the first three being called Major, the rest Minor). These books make exceedingly interesting, though at times admittedly obscure, reading. The subject matter is surprisingly diversified, even within the same book. Too, most of these books were assembled from speeches made by the prophets, and not always put together in the best order (e.g. the call of Isaiah is only recorded in chapter 6).

Amos, perhaps the earliest of the writing prophets (ca. 750 B.C.) is deeply concerned with social justice in the northern kingdom (even though he came from, and returned to, the south). He thoroughly castigates the social vices that plague societies of all times—greed, lack of consideration for the small operator, latifundism, etc. Amos is outspoken in his criticisms, mentioning those "who turn justice into gall" (5, 7), those "who sell the innocent for silver" (2, 6), and promising a "famine upon the land; not a famine of bread . . . but for hearing the words of Yahweh" (8, 11). It is hard to read the utterances of this conscientious man without seeing ourselves reflected in the mirror of his book.

Hosea, with all his marital sorrow, speaks of Yahweh's love for his people (the husband-wife symbolism is strongly brought out in this book) in terms that are surprisingly tender and beautiful —and will surely undermine the often asserted notion that there is only fear in the Old Testament! Read chapter 11 of Hosea and see for yourselves how the prophet's own willingness to take back the adulterous Gomer is a figure of Yahweh's great and merciful love for his faithless bridal people.

Isaiah mixed easily among the kings and court officials, yet not hesitating to present the policies that alone are suited to a theocratic society. Entangling alliances, trust in men, human measures, are for him not only doubtful politics but evils. "Zion shall be redeemed in judgment, and her converts in righteousness (1, 27). . . . If you do not hold fast (by faith) surely you shall not remain steadfast" (7, 9).

Jeremiah sees no real hope against the invasion from the north. For him the only policy is one of taking the punishment that he can only see as inevitable. He might be termed the most unpopular of all the prophets, for his message was the least pleasant. His was a disagreeable, unappreciated work, but he went on with it, and perhaps died in Egypt believing that he had been an absolute failure. Later generations of Jews held him in the highest regard (cf. 2 Macc 15, 12-16; Mt 16, 14).

Malachi may be called the prophet of genuine worship. He has much to say about worship "in spirit and in truth" and is anxious that God be given the adoration and praise of which he is worthy. He criticizes the priests in the strongest language for their lack of cult loyalty and wants to see the purification of the sons of Levi. The last of the writing prophets, he seems to have flourished around 450 B.C. The age that followed was largely a wisdom-age, though Hebrews never ceased hoping for the great prophet of Dt 18, 15-18. We note several places in 1 Maccabees where the priests are unable to make decisions and wait for some prophet to come and give them guidance (4, 46; 14, 41).

It is John the Baptist who breaks the prophetic silence after some four hundred years. So important was he considered that the primitive Gospel instructions always began with the account of his precursory work. His was the unique mission not merely to speak about a coming Redeemer—whether as prophet, king, priest, deliverer, or Suffering Servant; he was able to present the One in whom all these offices converge—who himself was the greatest of all the prophets of all times, who not only had the word of God, but *was* (and is) the Word of God.

Prophets are spoken of in the New Testament after the ascension of Christ, sometimes as foretelling the future (e.g. Agabus in Acts 21, 10), but more often as having the special charism to speak in enthusiastic, yet not always comprehensible, language (cf. 1 Cor 12–14).

The prophets never cease to be relevant. They deserve our attention as much today as at any other time. We can always learn from them, and every fresh reading gives us something more. We need to read the prophets—*not* in order to see if we can figure out some interesting dates about the future of the world and of mankind (Daniel and the Apocalypse have especially been subjected to this abuse)—a practice that inevitably ends in dismal failure and embarrassment for those that think they have worked out a foolproof system—but in order that we can better know, and become sensitive to, the will of God.

Prophecy has not utterly disappeared in our own times—though the delicate task of separating the authentic from the spurious is as much with us as it was with the Hebrews of old. We have our prophets—those who are so attuned to the workings of God's will and providence that they do not hesitate to deliver us a message, offering us guidance amidst bewilderment and light amidst darkness. The Church herself, as the continuation of Christ in the world, has a prophetic function, and she has never hesitated to use it—as unpopular as it might make her. When everyone condones wrong, she must still call it wrong; when all deny basic religious truth, she must affirm it. She has the Word of God within her because she is nothing else than Christ and his incorporated members. Thus Israel's mighty prophets have their counterpart in the New Israel—and the Old Testament has an additional reason for being everlastingly valuable and significant.

Those desirous of good books on this subject in English will enjoy *God's Heralds*, by Joseph Chaine.[2] Father John L. McKenzie's masterly *Two-Edged Sword*, to which we have frequently referred, has excellent material on the prophets scattered over

[2] Trans. by Brendan McGrath, O.S.B. (New York, Wagner, 1955).

several chapters (especially 2, 8, 9, 10, 11). And, most recently, Bruce Vawter, C.M., presents us with a masterly treatment of the prophets in *The Conscience of Israel.*[3]

19   *ISRAEL'S PURSUIT OF WISDOM*

LONG BEFORE the prophetical period came to a close with Malachi (around 450 B.C.) another important movement had begun in Israel. This was the cultivation of wisdom, and it can be traced back at least as far as King Solomon (about 961–922). This king was noted for his ability to recite wise sayings and to make wise decisions. "Wisdom, too, God gave to Solomon, and great discernment, and a store of knowledge wide as the sand on the sea-shore. For that, no king of the east or of Egypt could vie with him, of all men the wisest. . . . no nation round about but had heard of his fame. Three thousand parables king Solomon uttered, and of songs he made a thousand and five; and he discoursed of all the trees there are, from the cedar on Lebanon to the hyssop that grows out from the wall; and of beasts, and birds, and creeping things, and fish" (I Kgs 4, 29–34, Knox). Solomon's wisdom also made the deepest impression on the queen of Sheba, who, as we have said, came to establish trade relations with him (1 Kgs 10, 6–9). Yet, despite these glowing descriptions, Solomon's wisdom must have been rather shallow, for he was ensnared into idolatry by his innumerable wives, many of them devotees of other gods; and his ad-

[3] New York, Sheed & Ward, 1961.

ministration, as we saw earlier, was really an empty display bought at the exploitation of his subjects.

As time went on, however, it was Solomon's name that hovered over all pursuit of wisdom in Israel, and for a long time the bulk of wisdom-writing in the Old Testament was attributed to him. We now know that Solomon wrote but a small part of the inspired wisdom literature, but he probably had a good deal to do with the wisdom movement and may be regarded as a kind of patron-author of many parts of these books.

It is customary to speak of the seven Wisdom (sapiential) books of the Old Testament. These are Proverbs, Psalms, Job, Canticle of Canticles, Qoheleth, Ben Sirah and the book of Wisdom—listed approximately in their chronological order of composition. Though the final edition of some of these books is late, their origins go back many centuries earlier into Israelite history. This is especially true of Proverbs and Psalms. The last two books in our list are not found in Jewish or Protestant Bibles, though the Catholic Church has declared them inspired and canonical.

The term "Wisdom books" has its point, but the classification is a general one, and the books vary greatly among themselves. Some of them treat other subjects besides wisdom, and there is wisdom-writing in the Old Testament elsewhere than in these books. The Canticle, for example, is in some ways an unusual book to place in this section. Only a few of the psalms fall within the wisdom category. Job and Qoheleth courageously tackle some of man's greatest problems and thus differ from the more common tendency of Proverbs and Ben Sirah simply to pass on "traditional" thought. The book of Wisdom savors of the Hellenistic world of Alexandria and contains many approaches quite proper to itself. What we are trying to say is that we should not look for too much of a single stamp upon the Wisdom books of the Old Testament.

Israel was not the only ancient oriental nation to pursue wisdom. Egypt was also known for this, and in our times we have discovered some remarkable similarities between certain Proverbs and the wisdom sayings of Amen-em-Ope. Nor need we believe that Israel surpassed all others in every respect in her wisdom-endeavours. While the sapiential books are most rewarding, they fail to provide answers to many problems that we might think they should solve. Again, while Greek philosophers and Christian sages developed very abstract notions of wisdom (delving into the ultimate causes of all things), Hebrew wisdom remained much simpler. It was often little more than the ability to get along with others and make one's way in the world; or the knowledge of some craft (Exod 31, 3); or, at a higher level, the good sense to find in the observance and study of God's Law the only satisfying activity in human life. The book of Proverbs is notably lacking in supernatural motivation for its wisdom maxims. In the Canticle, the name of God occurs but once (and this very doubtfully, in 8, 6, where the term "flames of Yah" may simply mean "furious flames," as the Chicago Bible takes it). Having had the benefit of the Great Wise Man, Christ, and having been schooled by the great Christian wisdom seekers, St. Augustine and St. Thomas Aquinas, we may at times be disappointed with the simple aphorisms, the hesitant gropings, the earthy character or Hebrew wisdom. Yet Hebrew wisdom is extremely important and, apart from its own inherent contributions, can make us realize how much we have been benefited by the Christian revelation.

The book of Proverbs grew up over a period of some five hundred years, and this is even hinted at by the headings over the various collections within the book. The large collections, from 10, 1 to 22, 16 and from 25, 1 to 29, 27, are attributed to Solomon. The setting for the book is principally the royal court, though many proverbs undoubtedly grew up elsewhere and were transplanted into this atmosphere. The horizons of the writers are limited: they seldom reckon with retribution in a future life, for their knowledge of the future life (except in the book of Wisdom) is hazy and insecure; they customarily adhere to a system of retribution in this life which for them seems to work infallibly (though the author of Job knew that it did not). Proverbs teaches various virtues—among them "the fear of the Lord," which is the beginning of wisdom. This fear of the Lord is something like humility, an honest appraisal of one's self before the all-wise God. Proverbs includes a classic description of the Ideal Wife in 31, 10–31 (nor does it mince words about avoiding the company of evil women). The ideal wife is praised for her domestic virtues and competence—no small thing. Those who take time to read and meditate Proverbs in a good translation will come to enjoy the homely and profound wisdom that is found there.

Since the Psalms deserve special treatment, we will pass them over here.

The book of Job is not as simple as one might think. In fact, the more one reads this truly great classic, the more one comes to respect the wisdom that it contains and the difficulty of getting its full meaning. The book was completed around the beginning of the fifth century B.C. It went through a complicated literary process. Many scholars believe that the prose story at the beginning and end once existed separately and was used as a framework for what now lies within the book (in poetry), and that various other adjustments were made before our present book emerged. Though there may well have been an historical character named Job, we need not regard the account as historical. The book is didactic, and merely uses Job as a concrete way of working out a thorny problem, that of the innocent sufferer.

The reader knows from the Prologue that Job is blameless, and so realizes the special significance of the book. Job's friends, Eliphaz, Bildad, and Zophar, represent the traditional viewpoint: anyone who suffers must have committed some personal sin, and they push this view to the extreme. Thus the author reduces the traditional principle to absurdity, for he knew that it did not work—and he presses for some better solution, which neither he nor we can give in its entirety, although we have more revelation to guide us in our deliberations than he had— for he lacked our clear knowledge of eternal life. Chapter 19, 25– 27 presents a high point in the dialogue, for here Job makes a supreme act of faith in God and God's justice: "This at least I know, that one lives on who will vindicate me, rising up from the dust when the last day comes. Once more my skin shall clothe me, and in my flesh I shall have sight of God. I myself, with my own eyes; it will not be something other than myself that sees him. Deep in my heart is this hope reposed" (Knox). These lines have been made to proclaim belief in bodily resurrection— which they probably do not proclaim at all (the text is very un- certain), but they do proclaim great faith in God as Job's Vin- dicator. In certain straitened circumstances of life, this is all we can do, even after the Christian revelation.

The Canticle of Canticles (i.e. the *best* Song) is the shortest of the Wisdom books. It was probably written late in the fifth century B.C., and it has enjoyed high respect among both Jews and Christians. The famous Rabbi Akiba stated in the second century A.D. that "the world itself is not worth the day on which this book was given to Israel." This is indeed a powerful (if hyperbolic) commendation; yet the book may prove a pitfall for unprepared readers, and for this reason many interpreters felt obliged to lay great stress on its "higher" meaning. The Canticle will assuredly make a good deal of sense to its average reader—but the question is: What is its *intended* meaning? Is it an allegory (based on the thought found in the prophet Hosea) of Yahweh's love for his people, and hence, in the Christian interpretation, of Christ's love for his Church, or even for his immaculate Mother? Does everything in the book have a double meaning, literal and spiritual, or is there merely a general higher meaning to the entire book? Or again, is it simply a collection of chaste love poems, without any particular progress, showing the wonders of genuine admiration and love that man and woman, Bridegroom and Bride, have for one another? This latter interpretation is slowly gaining ground among recent Catholic writers. A. M. Dubarle, O.P., J. P. Audet, O.P., and Jacques Winandy, O.S.B., have all presented such an interpretation during the past few years. "The song is a mutual exchange of declarations of love and fidelity between two betrothed" is the remark of Father Roland E. Murphy, O.Carm., a leading American scholar who has studied and written about the Canticle for years.

Only those unfamiliar with the Old Testament and the Hebrew mentality would object to the book, so interpreted, being included in the Old Testament. Marriage was not considered unholy by the Hebrews—quite the contrary. The J writer in Gen 2, 23–24 and again in 3, 16 wonderfully describes the relationship between man and woman—without, of course, considering such a thing as a dedicated life of celibacy. While we cannot categorically exclude the higher marriage symbolism from the book, neither can we be sure that it is present; and if it is not present, the book need not embarrass us.

Qoheleth (the Preacher, the Assembler?) is one of the strangest books in the Bible. Not a few readers have wondered how it ever found its way into the sacred Canon. Is not its author a blasphemous skeptic? Does he not sow the seeds of doubt all around him? The answer to both of these questions is in the negative. Qoheleth is rather a daring thinker, one who is willing to set down his serious reflections on some of the enigmas of life. There is always need of men who test the foundations of traditional thought, and Qoheleth is one of them. Whoever Qoheleth was, he certainly was not Solomon, but some pseudonymous writer of the third century B.C. who was not willing to accept maxims without proving them against the background of experience; and he saw many difficulties, as had the author of Job, in answers that were too often complacent and simply did not work out in practice. "All is vanity and a chase after wind" is his reactionary remark. We need not believe that everything Qoheleth said was intended as a "final word." There is a good possibility that many of his observations are best understood in the context of musings—he himself is puzzled and is merely groping for an answer, guided by the very limited revelation of his time. Even the pursuit of wisdom has its vain side: ". . . much wisdom, much woe; who adds to learning, adds to the load we bear" (1, 18, Knox). We need not agree entirely, but there is some truth in this reflection.

Qoheleth has even been regarded as a materialist, for in 3, 19–21 he seems to class men and beasts together: "After all, man comes to the same ending as the beasts; there is nothing to choose between his lot and theirs; both alike are doomed to die. They have but one principle of life; what has man that the beasts have not? Frustration everywhere; we are all making for the same goal; of earth we were made, and to earth we must return. Who has the right to tell us that the spirit of man mounts upwards, and the spirit of a beast sinks down to the depth?" (Knox). Whatever else this is, it is not speculative philosophy. Qoheleth is not denying the existence of a "spiritual soul" since the ancient Hebrews had no such concept. They did not affirm that man is made up of "body and soul." They looked upon man as a unity, and were they to define man (which they never did), they would have called him an animated body. When man dies, his life-breath (cf. Gen 2, 7) leaves him, just as the life-breath of an animal leaves the animal. Nor can we discern where this breath goes—up or down. It cannot justly be stated that Qoheleth affirms the equality of nature between man and beast, for this would be entirely foreign to Hebraic thought (note the first chapter of Genesis on this point). Only man is created "to the image and likeness of God." All that Qoheleth states (and in this he is quite correct) is that as far as *appearances* are concerned, man and beast have a like end. Having no revelation of a blessed immortality to work with, he can only say that man dies and decays—as does the animal: "The dust returns to the earth as it once was, and the life-breath returns to God who gave it" (12, 7).

Those who feel just a little cynical will find solace in Qoheleth. Those also who enjoy the honest musings of an objective thinker cannot fail to appreciate both the thoughts of this unusual inspired writer and the tremendous benefits of Christianity. Qoheleth serves as a good preparation for the Christian revelation.

Ben Sirah is a long book, offering a great variety of information. The author is something of a snob, having travelled, having had the leisure for scribal study, and tending to look down on the man not so blessed. Yet there is much here for profitable reading, and the long praise of the "Fathers" from chapter 44 on is an interesting summary of Hebrew history in the form of minute biographies.

The last of the Wisdom books is called the book of Wisdom, and was written in Greek in Egypt by someone who had felt the impact of Greek philosophical thought. The book contains in chapters 10 to the end what we can only call "midrash"— reflection upon and a reinterpretation and reapplication of the great events of the Old Testament. Wisdom was written late, probably around 50 B.C., and offers many a fine piece of advice and much insight into Hebrew history. Its highly developed doctrine on reward and punishment in the next life is most refreshing and marks a distinct departure from the ordinary Old Testament doctrine.

Hebrew wisdom is a many-sided thing, and always had something of an air of mystery about it. If it is imperfect in many respects, it is nonetheless most valuable and we can profit from it. The wisdom movement did not die with the

Old Testament. It was carried on in wondrous manner in the New Testament writings. It should be carried on today within our hearts as we reflect on the meaning of life and work out our problems according to the will of God.

We recommend most highly the recent volume of Father Roland E. Murphy, O.Carm., *The Seven Books of Wisdom*[1] as well as Volume III of the Confraternity translation of the Old Testament (an outstanding piece of work by real experts). The highly valuable volume of J. L. McKenzie, S.J., *The Two-Edged Sword*, has three chapters (12-14) dealing with the Wisdom books and their thought. Most recently, the *Paulist Pamphlet Bible Series* has published *Proverbs*, with text and commentary by J. T. Forestell, C.S.B., and the other Wisdom books will follow.

Here is an area of Old Testament study worthy of our earnest investigation. We can be sure of deriving immense profit and joy from whatever effort we expend in the pursuit of wisdom.

20 *ISRAEL'S SACRED SONGS*

IF WE CAN BELIEVE St. Jerome (died 419-20), "the Church's greatest Doctor in the interpretation of Sacred Scripture," there was a time when the Christian faithful were so familiar with the Psalms that the plowman in the field and the workman in his shop sang them as they went about their toil. Medieval

[1] Milwaukee, Bruce, 1960.

piety, according to John Lenhart, O.F.M. Cap.,[1] was marked by a heavy use of the Psalms—not just among the clergy and religious, but among the faithful as well. We must confess that present-day Catholic piety in the West makes little room for such spontaneous devotional use of the Psalms. One might even venture the wry observation that most Latin-rite priests are not genuinely enthusiastic about the Psalms, though these psalms make up the substance of their prayer-life, viz. the Divine Office, which they recite in the name of the entire Church. Nor can we say, in all honesty, that the Psalter is without its problems, for all experience the pinch of trying to adapt themselves to its mentality. Let us look into this important Old Testament book.

The psalms—one hundred and fifty of them—make up a large collection (really three collections arranged into five "books"). These psalms, like many other parts of the Old Testament that we have inspected, did not grow up overnight. They are the accumulation of centuries. They were written by various men, or schools, at various times, for various reasons, treating of various themes, and they are of various lengths, and were at times recast to fit new situations. Generally speaking, they have a rich *prayer value*. St. Jerome was so convinced of this that his advice to Laeta, one of his spiritual daughters, was that he who takes up the study of Sacred Scripture should first of all learn the Psalms and thus learn how to pray. Too, the Psalms are something of a compendium of *all Old Testament thought* and give us a marvellous insight into the life and thinking of the Chosen People.

Just as any nation has its favorite, time-honored songs, so did the Israelites, God's Chosen People, have their sacred, divinely inspired songs. These they sang as a part of their liturgy (many of the psalms arose through, or were adapted to,

[1] Cf. "The Bible: the Popular Prayer-Book of the Pre-Reformation Laity," in *American Ecclesiastical Review*, 78 (1928), pp. 225–44.

liturgical use); they sang these psalms, too, in their tents, in the most divers circumstances of life, often using some simple musical accompaniment. The psalms take us right into the heart of the Israelites and—a thing of great significance—they were used by Our Lord, Our Lady, and many of the saints as the most intimate and satisfying expression of their piety. The Church at an early date took over the Songs of Zion for didactic, devotional, and liturgical use, and she has no intention of relinquishing them (from the Divine Office, Mass, and Ritual), no matter what our estrangement from them may be. The day may come when they will be liturgically given to us in our own tongue, and perhaps then we will once more learn to savor them as did the men and women of past ages.

We habitually think of David as the great psalm-writer, the "Royal Psalmist." That he wrote some of the psalms himself is absolutely certain (seventy-three are attributed to him in the psalm titles—though these titles are at times open to discussion). That David did not write all the psalms is equally certain. We might best think of David as a kind of patron-author with whose spirit the entire Psalter is stamped. When the New Testament cites a psalm "of David"—even when the speaker is Christ—this is not an absolute argument for Davidic authorship in the strict sense of the term. Authorship had a much wider significance in Hebrew antiquity than it has now, and is, at all events, of secondary importance.

What really matters is to understand the background, the literary types, the meaning, and the rich theology of the Psalms.

The psalmists, like other Hebrew writers, never thought of defining their God in formal terms. They rather spoke of him in the most graphic and concrete language. Yahweh is the Rock; the Lawgiver; the Shield; the Refuge; the Hope, and is given a score of other equally expressive titles. He is the God of Mercy, of Might, and of Deliverance, who chose the Israelites to be his very own, who lavished on them a whole

series of marvellous signs and wonders (interventions in their
national life); who gave them the Law as the standard of
Covenant love; and who asks for their fidelity and loyalty.

It is Yahweh, too, who promised through Nathan (2 Sm 7,
11ff.; Ps 89) to perpetuate the Davidic line, to raise up eventually
a Davidic monarch of the greatest stature. The Messianic
Psalms dwell on this theme and thus have a relationship to
Christ and Christianity that puts them in a class apart.

We are forced to admire the psalmists for a number of
reasons. One of them is their willingness to spend time *simply
adoring God,* praising him, proclaiming his grandeur and works:
"See how the skies proclaim God's glory, how the vault of
heaven betrays his craftsmanship! Each day echoes its secret
to the next, each night passes on to the next its revelation of
knowledge" (Ps 18 [19], 1–2, Knox). In our times, when prayer
for many people means no more than petition, and very personal petition, we can derive a tremendous lesson in prayer from
the Psalms. The Hebrews asked for things, even very personal
things, but they did not stop there, and they probably did not
start there either. Greater concerns first won their attention.
They praised God, they expressed sorrow for their sins, they
implored the mercy of God. "Blessed be the living Lord who
is my refuge, praised be the God who delivers me!" (17 [18], 47,
Knox). "Let the whole world keep holiday in God's presence,
sing praise to his name, pay homage to his glory!" (65 [66],
1, 2, Knox).

But, let us be frank about the matter. The psalms are basically
Hebrew prayers. They are often limited in perspective to the
Hebrew outlook. Their authors do not hesitate at times to pour
out the liveliest curses upon the national and personal enemy,
wishing him the direst evils. ". . . let him leave the court of
judgment a doomed man, pleading with heaven in vain. Swiftly
let his days come to an end, and his office be entrusted to another; orphancy for the children, widowhood for the wife!"

(108 [109], 7-9 Knox). Too, the psalms can at times be very nationalistic and narrow in viewpoint, though this may be more easily excused since Israel *was* the chosen nation. As we go through the psalms it is impossible to miss these imperfections, though they are not found everywhere, nor do they make up anything like the greater part of the Psalter.

The psalms, too, are limited in their view of the future life. References that seem to point to a blessed eternity often have another meaning, for during the age in which the psalms were composed the Hebrews had a very hazy notion of the next world, Sheol being the one concept with which they most frequently and confidently dealt—and to this darksome abode no one wished to go. ". . . . my heart is full of trouble. My life sinks ever closer to the grave; I count as one of those who go down into the abyss, like one powerless" (87 [88], 3-5, Knox).

The Christian is sometimes at a loss to know what to do with some passages of the psalms: ". . . blessed be the man who will catch up thy children, and dash them against the rocks!" (136 [137], 9, Knox). Such an exclamation should not fit the Christian's and certainly does not fit Christ's spirit.

There are those who use all kinds of subtleties to escape these embarrassments and take refuge in accommodated meanings (which are really not scriptural meanings at all). The problem is not an easy one, but I cannot share the view of those who see Christ *everywhere* in the Psalms—either being spoken to, or speaking to us, or being spoken of, etc. That such an outlook is valid on occasion is quite admissible—but it is hardly tenable that all the psalms are really Christocentric to this extent in their genuine literal or higher meaning. If we wish to accommodate their meaning, we must call it accommodation, advised Pius XII in his 1943 encyclical. But if we wish to bring out their root literal meaning, then we must be prepared to admit that the psalms speak at times in a manner quite at odds with the Christian outlook, or fail to carry the heavy meaning that is extracted from them. As edifying as it may be to sing Ps 23 as a sacramental hymn (baptism, the Eucharist, confirmation, etc.), such is hardly the real meaning of the psalm, whether we speak of its literal or fuller sense. Does this mean that we can't pray the psalms as Christians? By no means. In many cases the prayer value is so profound that no transposition of any kind need be made. At times, however, it will mean thinking to ourselves that *we* cannot share the sentiments of Hebrew hate and revenge, and thus we will have to transpose the basic thought of the psalms. In many cases there is a genuine "deeper sense" or typology involved in the psalms, so that Old Testament values can almost automatically be applied (validly) by the Christian to New Testament realities: manna-Eucharist; Old Covenant-New Covenant; earthly Jerusalem-heavenly Jerusalem; Yahweh's kindness and fidelity fulfilled in the redemptive work of Christ; Old Law-New Law; joy over an earthly deliverance and joy over an eternal deliverance, etc. There is no end to these valid higher meanings that we can see throughout the psalms.

This writer, however, cannot do otherwise than Pius XII counsels in his encyclical of 1943, viz. to seek out, always and everywhere, first of all the sense of Scripture which is called literal—that meaning which arises not only from the words of Scripture but from the intention of the inspired human author, God's intrument. Doing this, we will always begin with what is firm and solid and can then build securely and wisely upon a reliable foundation.

Present-day scholarship both outside and inside the Catholic Church has spent a good deal of effort trying to classify the various kinds of psalms. This is an extremely valuable step in our psalm study and psalm praying. The following major literary divisions among the psalms (according to the writings of Hermann Gunkel) have been made: *Hymns* (or songs of

Praise); *Community Lamentations; Royal Psalms* (including Messianic Psalms); *Personal Lamentations;* and *Personal Thanksgivings.* To these more general classifications the following more particular types may be added: Blessings and Curses; Pilgrim Psalms; National Thanksgivings; Legends; Psalms dealing with the Law; Prophetic Psalms; and Wisdom Psalms (cf. J. L. McKenzie, S.J., *The Two-Edged Sword*[2]). Many of the psalms fall into two or more of these divisions, for it is characteristic of the psalms to shift from one subject to another—at times the result of originally separate songs having been combined.

Other nations in oriental antiquity besides the Israelites had their songs too, and we can hardly imagine that Israel was utterly uninfluenced by them. However, as in the case of the early chapters of Genesis, Israel rarely borrowed without transposing, recasting, purifying, adapting, and sometimes counter-stating the matter at hand. Especially with regard to the royal-messianic psalms, we now realize that many verses, once thought to be clear attestations of the Messiah's divinity, such as "You are my son; this day have I begotten you" (Ps 2, 7), are really products of "court-style" language and signify no more than adoption by the deity of the monarch being enthroned. This does not exclude the New Testament's seeing a fuller sense in these and similar verses (cf. Heb 1, 5; 5, 5; Acts 13, 33).

We must admire the spirit of optimism and confidence that prevails throughout the psalms. Ps 88 is a notable exception—one of the gloomiest pieces of Old Testament writing. The Christian, tried though he may be, should find in the psalms a great uplifting force, for Christianity is basically optimistic in outlook.

To gain familiarity with the psalms we need to study them in a good translation, and we need instruction on their background. Much information may be found in Father McKenzie's

[2] P. 267.

The Two-Edged Sword, where one chapter, "The Prayer of the Hebrews," is devoted to the Psalms. In Father Roland E. Murphy's *Seven Books of Wisdom,* one chapter, "An Approach to the Psalms," is of the greatest value. Those who wish more detailed instruction may go through the two-volume work of Msgr. Edward J. Kissane;[3] or perhaps better, acquire the volume on the Psalms (now being translated) by the Dutch Trappist, Pius Drijvers. Those who read French will find tremendous help in the three-volume work by Pierre Guichou, *Les Psaumes Commentés par la Bible.*[4]

We cannot gain acquaintance with the psalms overnight. It takes time and patience slowly and thoroughly to assimilate the genuine meaning and valid deeper meanings of Israel's Sacred Songs.

21 SOME LATE BOOKS OF THE OLD TESTAMENT

READERS WHO HAVE patiently persevered with us know by this time that the Old Testament is made up of a whole library of surprisingly different books—many of which we have already examined. Before leaving the Old Testament, there are a few more books that merit our attention. Some of these books will only be found in Catholic Bibles (Tobit, a portion of Daniel, the Maccabees, and Judith); others are found in both

---

[3] *The Book of Psalms,* trans. from a critically revised Hebrew text, with a Commentary (Westminster, Newman, 1953).

[4] Paris, Editions du Cerf.

Jewish and Protestant Bibles (Jonah and most of Daniel). Though Wisdom was probably the latest book in the (Catholic) Old Testament, we have already considered it along with the Wisdom literature. In this matter of the formation of the Old Testament, we cannot recommend too highly (or too often) the inexpensive chart, ingeniously arranged, by Father Sebastiano Pagano, O.M.I., called a *Chronological Table of the Books of the Old Testament.* The study of this Table is an education in itself.

In some ways Jonah has proved to be the most misunderstood book in the Old Testament library. Written around the year 400 B.C. by an unknown author of great perception and universalist outlook—one whom we might term an Old Testament "ecumenist"—Jonah is really a clever satire on a Jewish outlook that we can only label as narrow, snobbish, and complacent. The author makes use of the *name* of an eighth-century prophet, Jonah (cf. 2 Kgs 14, 25), to represent this outlook, and the now fictionalized Jonah will go to almost any extreme to escape the task of sharing the Word of God with those outside of Israel. Having finally succeeded in winning the Ninevites to repentance (even the animals!), though he did everything to avoid his mission, Jonah is afflicted with the deepest grief—*for this is not what he wanted.* When one reads the book as a satire, it takes on tremendous meaning.

The short evaluation given by Father McKenzie in *The Two-Edged Sword* shows about as profound an appreciation of Jonah as one could wish. "It was no ordinary Hebrew who could look at the capital city of the piratical Assyrians, stuffed with treasure looted from their subjects, served by the slaves they had captured, and see in its proud people ignorant 'little ones,' demanding the compassion of the Lord. He was a Hebrew who had looked into the heart of the God of Hebrew belief and Hebrew tradition, and told what he saw. As the Lord had compassion on Israel, so He must have compassion on all whom

He had made. If we think the Hebrews were narrow, let us remember that there were those among them who could rise to a view of humanity almost as broad as the view of the Lord Himself, from whom they learned it."[1]

We can only regret that our attention in studying Jonah was diverted for so long a time into the special issue of whether a whale (we are not sure that the "great fish" really was a whale) could swallow a man. Jonah is not a "fish story," though it is fiction. It is parabolic fiction and has amazing significance.

The James Bartley story, a sailor's yarn if there ever was one, has been brought up by many a conscientious teacher (including myself in younger years) to prove that Jonah was actually swallowed by a whale and could live to tell about it. For some reason "historicity" has preoccupied our attention in biblical studies to a distorted degree. Our first question is nearly always: Did it really happen? Rarely do we ask the question that Semites loved to ask: *What does it mean?* In point of fact, by the time this book was written, Nineveh, destroyed in 612, was a memory only, and an exaggerated one at that.

The details of this story make it fantastic when we begin to press for historicity. The author, to all appearances, strove to provide details which Jewish readers would so certainly recognize as exaggeratedly *unhistorical* that they would grasp the full impact of the satire. The author wanted to shout to the complacent and narrow-minded: *"You* are like Jonah."

Jonah marks a summit in Old Testament writing and is decidedly reactionary to the narrow outlook of Ezra and Nehemiah. Though he himself was saved through divine mercy, Jonah's attitude is stingy when he sees it shown to others: "Great pity thou hast, the Lord said, for yonder ivy-plant, that was not of thy growing, and no toil cost thee; a plant that springs in a night, and in a night must wither! And what

[1] Pp. 202-3.

of Nineve? Here is a great city, with a hundred and twenty thousand folk in it, and none of them can tell right from left, all these cattle, too; and may I not spare Nineve?" (4, 10–11, Knox). The writer comes very close to a genuine Christian universalism—which, we must confess, we do not always possess ourselves!

Another didactic book of the Old Testament is the story of Tobit, which has come down to us in several variant Greek editions, and which has turned up at Qumrân in partially preserved Hebrew and Aramaic texts. This book was most probably written between 300 and 400 B.C., and it brings out many of the features of ideal family life, so treasured by good Jewish people of all times. The elder Tobit is a model of Jewish piety and goodness. His son, Tobias, is an ideal son as well as a perfect husband for the much-tried Sarah, who had lost seven husbands, apparently because of their faulty attitude towards marriage.

The story is a delightful one but becomes ridiculous when subjected to purely historical analysis—as was so often done in earlier times. Tobit has probably only a small historical kernel, but its didactic value is great. From beginning to end the book is instructive. It shows marked relationship with the Story and Sayings of Ahiqar. Though possibly written by a Jew of the (Egyptian?) Diaspora, the story is situated in Mesopotamia. The wonderful kindness of the archangel Raphael (spoken of only in this book of the Bible) is representative of the all-benevolent providence of God.

The book of Daniel is found in the Hebrew Bible, but not among the Prophets! It was written *too late* to be included in that section of the Hebrew Bible and was hence placed in the final section: the *Writings*. Daniel probably came out in its final form between 167 and 164—much later than a casual reading of it would suggest. For us, Daniel has the distinction of being found in three original languages—parts of it being in Hebrew, parts in Aramaic, and parts (those not accepted by Jews and Protestants) in Greek. To read this book in its original tongues demands more than average linguistic ability.

But it is not merely the linguistic question that singles out Daniel as an unusual book of the Bible. Its very contents, quite diversified, make it extremely difficult to interpret. There is a narrative section, chapters 1—6, which most readers will be able to follow without great struggle. Here, the prophet Daniel, taken as captive to the court of Nebuchadnezzar in Babylon, wins the admiration of all for his unusual abilities—dream-interpreting and lion-taming—and his unbounded faith in God. The stories were perhaps at one time circulated independently and follow something of a pattern. Daniel is persecuted; then wins the king's favor through his abilities and integrity; and is raised to honor, with Nebuchadnezzar acknowledging the supremacy of Daniel's God, Yahweh. These stories are of the greatest interest—many of them now classics (e.g. the writing on the wall in 5, 5ff.)—but they are hardly history in the strict sense of the word. A number of discrepancies have been discovered which a rigidly historical writer could never have tolerated. Like the book of Daniel in general, these stories are aimed at showing that there is only one everlasting kingdom —the Kingdom of God. For this reason Daniel is heavily drawn upon in the New Testament, especially in Our Lord's sermon on the destruction of Jerusalem and in the Apocalypse.

Another section of Daniel (chapters 7—12) involves a series of *visions* of an apocalyptic nature. These visions actually describe through symbols many (already past) historical events —even in fine detail—but are most difficult to follow without a commentary. The general lesson, however, of the four visions is like that of the six stories in chapters 1—6; viz., that persecutors pass away along with their kingdoms, but Yahweh will triumph over them for ever. The Kingdom of God is coming. The book aims at providing hope and consolation to those suffering the dire persecution (167–164) organized by Antiochus IV Epiphanes, monarch of the Greek Seleucid Kingdom.

The "Catholic" parts of Daniel include the song of the Three Youths in the Fiery Furnace (3, 24–90); the Story of Susanna (13); and the stories of Bel and the Dragon (14). The final chapter contains a large quantum of fiction.

Though a difficult book (and we have hardly scratched the surface), Daniel is also rewarding. Being late, it brings out a developed doctrine on eternal life and resurrection in chapter 12, 2–3: "Many shall wake, that now lie sleeping in the dust of earth, some to enjoy life everlasting, some to be confronted for ever with their disgrace. Bright shall be the glory of wise counsellors, as the radiance of the sky above; starry-bright for ever their glory, who have taught many the right way" (Knox).

Many of the narratives in Daniel are easily understood, and their lessons, once grasped, will not be easily forgotten. Daniel makes its own valuable contribution to the redemptive hope of the Old Testament. Here we find the "Son of Man" (7, 13)— a term that Christ preferred to use for himself. Here, too, is the famous though enigmatic prophecy of the seventy weeks, the cause of almost endless speculation, especially within certain fanatic sects. But it is the doctrine of the coming of God's Kingdom, supplanting all other kingdoms, that characterizes the whole book of Daniel.

The two books of Maccabees were written after the time of Daniel, though they go over some of the same ground. We speak of the first and second Maccabees, and the average student immediately concludes that second Maccabees begins where first Maccabees leaves off. Actually the two books are independent products, partially overlapping and not always in harmony with one another. The books are historical in the sense that they are concerned with historical matters, yet we must insist on our by now tiresome distinction that the history of the

Bible operates on principles differing from those of modern history writers. This is especially true of the second book, where the author is really making something of a plea for his people and is openly on their side in all that he writes. His type of writing has been called "sympathetic history," and that sums up its character very satisfactorily.

The Maccabees take us into a period of Jewish history otherwise not well represented in the Bible. Though details at times flood the stories, the general picture is one that can only prove rewarding and valuable. Religious lessons abound all the way through the books. The reference to an intermediate state after death (purgatory) in 2 Macc 12, 38ff., is perhaps the best biblical evidence available on this doctrine (since most of the references commonly alleged from the New Testament are not certain). This question was thoroughly discussed in the April 1960 *American Ecclesiastical Review* by Father Ernest Lussier, S.S.S.

One thing that will impress all readers of the Maccabees is the heroic resistance made by a section of the Jewish people against pagan infiltrations. Here is Judaism against Paganism, and we must admire the heroic outlook of the earlier Maccabees, with their sense of the sacred. The family later became notably corrupt.

The book of Judith (means "Jewess") was written somewhere around the year 100 B.C. It is the story of a heroic woman who saved the town of Bethulia (otherwise not famous) against the impending attack of one Holofernes, mighty warrior in the service of the neo-Babylonian monarch, Nebuchadnezzar. The story is a simple one, hinging on the beautiful and pious widow named Judith who vanquished Holofernes by her charms and cunning. That the book is largely fictional is admitted by most scholars today, but at the same time they point out the didactic value, for it shows the rewards of trust in God, his mastery of history and his power to vanquish any enemy. I have long suspected that Bethulia is a fictitious name, like that of the heroine, and that this city, with its priests, etc., stands for Jerusalem, or any typically Jewish fortress-city.

Reading the book of Judith may bring up a moral problem: viz., how could Judith, for all her piety and chastity, have been so cunning in her dealings with the enemy; and more especially, how could she have exposed herself to moral danger? We have the right to ask these questions, for they arise from refined Christian consciences. However, it is highly doubtful that such questions arose in the mind of the writer of the book. Judith, as the story goes, did take a risk, but she prayed and fortified herself by fasting, and this seemed sufficient.

Rarely will we find Christian moral standards presented in the Old Testament. To look for them is to look in vain. God is a patient pedagogue, and he has led men to Christian ideals only gradually—and any honest man knows that we don't always measure up to them. The learned Dominican Cardinal Cajetan (died in 1534) exclaimed in commenting on the Prima-Secundae of St. Thomas' *Summa Theologica* (q. 99, a. 6): "Alas, alas, how few today seem to belong to the status of the New Law! And would that we at least belonged to the status of the Old." Generally speaking, we can ill afford to point the accusing finger at the moral lapses of the Chosen People of old— whether these are found in fact or fiction.

There are vast areas of the Old Testament that we have not looked at in detail, nor was this our intention. We have seen many of the great and guiding themes of the Old Testament: how it arose; the various classes of books that make it up; the high-points of its history. I firmly believe—as every Christian *must* believe—that the Old Testament has an *everlasting value.* It marks a long and extremely important stage in God's plan of salvation.

Nor have the Hebrews ceased to be precious in the sight of God. The Jewish people are a people of mystery. Over them hovers the loving and protective hand of divine providence. "I must not fail, brethren, to make this revelation known to you; or else you might have too good a conceit of yourselves. Blindness has fallen upon a part of Israel, but only until the tale of the Gentile nations is complete; then the whole of Israel will find salvation. . . . In the preaching of the gospel, God rejects them, to make room for you; but in his elective purpose he still welcomes them, for the sake of their fathers; God does not repent of the gifts he makes, or of the calls he issues" (Rom 11, 25, 26; 28–30, Knox). It was after writing these lines that Paul exclaimed: "How deep is the mine of God's wisdom, of his knowledge; how incrutable are his judgments, how undiscoverable his ways!" (Rom 11, 33, Knox).

Anyone who spurns the Old Testament, or unduly criticizes it, knows neither the meaning of Christianity nor what it means personally to be a Christian.

22 THE MEANING OF THE QUMRÂN SCROLLS

BFORE WE LEAVE the Old Testament to take up the New, an "inter-testamental" phenomenon deserves our attention for the simple reason that it is *transitional*, situated between the two Testaments. This phenomenon may be summarized by the single word "Qumrân"—though we could speak of it more adequately as "Manuscript Discoveries in the Judaean Desert," for Qumrân is only one, though so far certainly the most important, place where ancient manuscripts have been found.

Already much has been written on Qumrân—enough to constitute a large library! Scores of various-sized books in many different languages, learned treatises and articles, and countless popularizations have gone through the press. There is even a French quarterly publication, *Revue de Qumrân,* exclusively devoted to scholarly studies on what are popularly called "The Dead Sea Scrolls." Not everything that has been published is of equal value—far from it; in fact, some of it is sensational, or even positively misleading, and has created a suspicious attitude in many minds regarding the Qumrân Scrolls. It is only gradually that this attitude is being dissipated by a powerful current of thought shared by top-ranking scholars of all persuasions. Nor is the story yet complete. Considerable material has yet to be analyzed, and new finds are still being made.

The discovery of this ancient material can only be called phenomenal. Twenty years ago the scholarly world would never have dreamed that such discoveries were possible; yet today, after fifteen years, we have become almost too accustomed to them. What we are going to say will represent an effort towards presenting in simplified form the most important features of the Qumrân story, based on the latest research of Qumrân scholars. For the sake of clarity, we will use a series of headings to introduce the various aspects of the question.

Circumstances of Discovery

It was in the spring of 1947 that the first scrolls were discovered in one of the many caves in the rugged cliffs that overlook the area known as Qumrân on the northwest shore of the Dead Sea. The discoverer, a fifteen-year-old Bedouin goatherd by the name of Mohammed the Wolf, had thrown a stone after one of his goats which had strayed into the twenty-six-foot-long cave, and upon hearing the clank of breaking pottery, he went into the cave to investigate. What he discovered was a series of tall jars from each of which was protruding a leather scroll wrapped up, mummy-like, in linen cloth.

After a long process of passing the scrolls on, trying to read them (the Hebrew script was foreign to the Arabic-speaking Bedouin) and to find out what they were, they were identified by various Semitic scholars in Jerusalem. Some of the scrolls turned out to be books of the Old Testament; others were peculiar commentaries on Old Testament books; still others were religious documents giving expression to the beliefs and hopes of some Jewish sect. As the identifications were made, e.g. the complete book of Isaiah by Jan van der Ploeg, O.P., in 1947, great interest was aroused, and soon expeditions were organized to make thorough investigations of the entire Qumrân region.

In eleven of the caves scroll material was found. Cave 4, discovered quite accidentally in 1952, yielded a greater variety of material than any other, though the material was more fragmentary than that found in Cave 1. When the Qumrân region was thoroughly scoured, other finds, of lesser importance, were made at Wadi Murabba'at, some twelve miles south of Qumrân, but still on the edge of the Sea; at Qirbet Mird, back in the Wadi en-Nar; and at the great rock fortress of Masada, much further south and somewhat back from the shore of the forty-six-mile-long Dead Sea.

In some cases materials were kept back by the Arabs and only turned in as they decided to sell them. Probably the Arabs have sold most of this material by now. Other finds are still being made here and there. The thousands of fragments of scroll material as well as the major scrolls all lie within the city of Jerusalem, whether in the Rockefeller Museum, the big center of decipherment and publication (Jordan side); or on the Israel side of the city, where the seven major scrolls are kept. The present plans seem to aim at keeping the material in Jerusalem, since the sales of various allotments to great centers of learning

(Heidelberg University, the Vatican Library, McGill University in Montreal, etc.) were all rescinded last year.

Inventory of the Scroll Material

A complete inventory of scroll material cannot yet be provided, since not all the scrolls have been identified, nor could we begin to list in this chapter all the items that have been identified. However, it may be stated that all the books of the Hebrew Old Testament, Esther alone excepted, have been discovered at Qumrân either in complete or fragmentary form, sometimes represented several times over. Some of the books not found in the Hebrew Bible but contained in the "Catholic" Bible, such as Tobit, have been found in fragmentary Hebrew or Aramaic texts—an interesting factor, as we pointed out earlier, in the study of the Canon of Sacred Scripture. Found, too, were some "commentaries" on the Old Testament books, such as those on Habakkuk and Genesis, both of which are heavily sectarian and/or fanciful. A large selection of what we call apocryphal books (termed "pseudepigrapha" by others) have also turned up. Then there are many documents that are sectarian in nature without reference directly to the Bible, such as the *Manual of Discipline,* the religious rule of a monastic group; the *War between the Children of Light and the Sons of Darkness;* and the *Hymns* (Hodayot), something like the Psalms. Many other documents of a purely civil nature, such as contracts, were also discovered.

Most of this material was written in Hebrew or Aramaic on leather or parchment. The Copper Scroll stands in a class by itself, for the writing was hammered into the copper, and it took very careful workmanship to cut the scroll into strips for decipherment (it could not be unrolled). Hasty excavations at some of the sites mentioned in this scroll (which turned out to be a fanciful catalogue of buried treasure) have yielded nothing so far (and probably never will), though John Marco Allegro went about the task with great enthusiasm. His book, *The Treasure of the Copper Scroll,* received at the hands of Père Roland de Vaux, O.P., in the January 1961 *Revue Biblique* one of the harshest reviews this writer has ever seen (and rightly so).

In summary we might say that some six hundred or more separate manuscripts have been represented in the Qumrân finds—some entirely complete, others in the most fragmentary condition.

How Old are the Scrolls?

Once the more important identifications were made, the crucial question of the age of the scrolls was taken up. Were they medieval forgeries, as a few scholars maintained (and still maintain)? Or did they date from around the beginning of the Christian era, as Dr. W. F. Albright asserted from the very beginning in words that have now become famous: "My heartiest congratulations on the greatest manuscript discovery of modern times! There is no doubt in my mind that the script is more archaic than that of the Nash Papyrus (2nd century A.D.). . . . I should prefer a date around 100 B.C. What an absolutely incredible find! And there can happily not be the slightest doubt in the world about the genuineness of the manuscript." (This remark was made by Dr. Albright from the United States after he had seen photostatic samples of the large Isaiah Scroll.)

The weight of opinion has surely fallen on the side of the antiquity of the scrolls. Men of the most varied background hold this view, while Professor Solomon Zeitlin doggedly adheres to a medieval dating.

Various arguments have led to the ancient dating for the scrolls. (We speak of the date at which the scrolls were *copied out*, not that of their original composition.) Of these, the argument based on paleography (the ancient style of writing) is highly influential. There is also the Carbon-14 dating, based on the ratio of carbon-loss by the linen wrappers (the scrolls themselves have never been subjected to this test). Though having a two-hundred-year plus or minus variant, this test has taken us back near to the beginning of the Christian era. The method has recently been perfected, as described by J. A. Fitzmyer, S.J.,[1] and now indicates a dating very close to 20 B.C.

Reconstructing the Origin of the Scrolls

Closely allied to, and intimately bound up with, the dating of the scrolls was the question of their origin. *How did they ever get into the caves where they were found?* In an effort to answer this question it seemed absolutely necessary to undertake the excavation of Qirbet Qumrân (i.e. Ruin of Qumrân), situated in the very area, and long thought to be an abandoned Roman fortress. This excavation was made, beginning in 1951, by the Jordan Department of Antiquities and the Dominican Fathers of the Ecole Biblique. The results were most rewarding. It was established beyond all doubt that the ruin was that of an ancient monastery of Jewish sectarians. The reconstruction was slowly but solidly made, various rooms, such as the scriptorium, being identified. Here was found a long table with the dried-up inkwells used by the sectarians in their scribal work. Today most authorities believe that the "monks" of Qumrân were Essenes, or closely related to them, and that the *Manual of Discipline* was nothing else than their religious Rule. (These Essenes were a Jewish sect of separatists and ascetics with strong interests in

[1] "The Date of the Qumrân Scrolls," *America*, 104 (March 18, 1961), pp. 780–81.

the Law, with apocalyptic hopes, and a conviction that they were the authentic people of God.)

Jars, such as those found in the caves, were found in the ruins of the monastery—also coins and other objects that aided dating. It has now been shown that the monastery was built somewhere around 135 B.C. and was used until around 31 B.C., when destruction by earthquake caused the site to be abandoned for some thirty or forty years. Under Herod Archelaus (4 B.C.—6 A.D.) the site was again inhabited and the monastery rebuilt. It was used by the sectarians until around June of the year 68 A.D., when it was destroyed by Roman military forces. The site was then used by Roman soldiers until about the year 100, and by Jewish insurgents from 132 to 135 A.D. After this it was finally abandoned.

There is, of course, the added question as to why the Essenes put their scrolls in the caves. A final answer cannot be given. Many think it was done in view of the expected invasion of the Roman troops in 68 A.D., with the idea that when the danger had passed the scrolls could be restored to the monastery; but the restoration never took place. Others have suggested that Qumrân was something of a central lending-library for the Essene communities in Palestine (ideal because of its dry climate), and that the scrolls were deposited in the caves when not in use.

Most Qumrân scholars believe that the scrolls were copied out around the beginning of the Christian era, some of them as far back as 100 B.C. or even earlier. In the case of books like Qoheleth this would take us back nearly to the time when the book was first written.

Work Remaining on the Scrolls

In the Rockefeller Museum in Old Jerusalem, Jordan, one wing is set off as the "scrollery." Here an international and interdenominational group works steadily at identifying, deciphering, and publishing the scrolls—all under the supervision of Dominican Père Roland de Vaux, Director of the Ecole Biblique, which is only a couple of blocks away. The goal is to publish all the scrolls in large quarto volumes, entitled *Discoveries in the Judaean Desert*. Volume I[2] of this series appeared in 1955 under the joint editorship of Dominic Barthélemy, O.P., and Jozef Milik; Volume II, containing most of the finds at Murabba'at, appeared in 1961.

No one knows when this work will be completed, since this depends on many factors. Some of the scrolls are hard to identify, and it would be ideal to make the identifications before publication. Nor is this a work that can be unduly hurried. It must be done thoroughly, patiently, and without injurious pressure on the workmen. This might be termed a real ecumenical project, and it has resulted in a much better inter-credal understanding all the way round, for the team of workmen naturally discuss countless theological problems as they advance in their work. Several American priests have served on the team thus far.

Are the Scrolls a Threat to Christianity?

Unfortunately, shortly after the first (and tentative) decipherments were made, the suggestion was put forth that the Dead Sea Scrolls would deal a death blow to our ideas about Christian origins. Such observations were due principally to the ex-priest, now professor at the Sorbonne, André Dupont-Sommer, who stated that Qumrân's Teacher of Righteousness was "an exact prototype of Jesus" and that "the Galilean Master, as he is presented to us in the writings of the New Testament, appears in many respects as an astonishing reincarnation of the Teacher of Righteousness." Though Professor Dupont-Sommer retracted many of his sensation-making statements later on, they were

2 New York, Oxford.

propagated in England by John Marco Allegro and in this country by Edmund Wilson. These men, incidentally, are good English stylists and turned out writings that became best-sellers. No wonder that it takes a long time to clear away the false impressions which they created, even though they themselves have changed their own opinion in the meantime. There is absolutely no reason why Christians should fear the Qumrân Scrolls. They are an entire blessing, and it is only a pity that irresponsible statements were made about them.

Positive Values of the Qumrân Discoveries

The Qumrân finds have contributed positively in numerous ways to biblical-archaeological studies. Most significantly, they have offered us texts of the Bible that are in some cases a thousand years older than the texts we had to work with before 1947. The Qumrân biblical texts stand in remarkable agreement with our hitherto critically established texts, only few and minor variations being found. In some cases Hebrew texts have turned up that have greater similarity to the Greek Septuagint translation (made in pre-Christian times) than to the Massoretic (vowel-equipped) Hebrew text. Hence the value of the Septuagint translation has been increasingly recognized.

The non-biblical scrolls have thrown immense light on the "inter-testamental" period (for which reason we are dealing with the scrolls here) and give us a much better picture of its messianic expectation, theological doctrine, and religious practices. Scholars have made countless efforts at confronting Qumrân doctrine with that of Christianity and have found both surprising similarities and even more surprising differences. Far from destroying the uniqueness of Christianity, Qumrân has helped us to see its remarkable superiority over other systems prevalent at that time. The concepts of charity, redemption, and messianism, to mention but a few, are much loftier and more clear-cut in the New Testament than in the Qumrân writings.

Qumrân has given us vast quantities of Hebrew and Aramaic writings with which to advance our knowledge of Semitic, and the archaeology of Qumrân is valuable as one more contribution to the background of the Bible.

What to Read on the Qumrân Scrolls

The mere listing of books and articles on the Scrolls is *now enough to fill one large volume!* Those who have only read Wilson, Dupont-Sommer, Allegro, A. Powell Davies, del Medico, or Zeitlin owe it to themselves to take up one of the following volumes: E. Sutcliffe, *Monks of Qumrân;*[3] Kurt Schubert, *The Dead Sea Community;*[4] Jan van der Ploeg, *The Excavations at Qumrân;*[5] Jozef T. Milik, *Ten Years of Discovery in the Wilderness of Judaea;*[6] or F. M. Cross, *The Ancient Library of Qumrân and Modern Biblical Studies.*[7]

The Qumrân discoveries are not merely fascinating in themselves, they are important to scriptural study, and we cannot dispense ourselves from getting more than a smattering of knowledge concerning them.

[3] Westminster, Newman, 1960.
[4] New York, Harper, 1959.
[5] New York, Longmans, 1958.
[6] Naperville, Ill.; Allenson, 1959.
[7] New York, Doubleday, 1958.

23 GOSPEL AND GOSPELS

JUST AS CHRIST HIMSELF is the great *sacrament* of the New Law from whom our seven sacraments derive their institution and power, so Christ's preaching of the message of salvation is the Good News—the Gospel—from which our four canonical Gospels take their rise and of which they are the marvellous and inspired expression. *There is only one Gospel:* the Gospel of Christ, and this Gospel, in the language of St. Paul, is "the saving power if God" (Rom 1, 16). St. Augustine once stated that "The Gospel springs from the mouth of Christ; and though he is now seated in heaven he still teaches on earth." It is not without good reason that our four canonical Gospels are each entitled ". . . according to Matthew; Mark; Luke; John"; for it is always *Christ's* Gospel *as presented* by his inspired evangelists.

We must stress the fact that the Gospel was first of all *oral* and the first Evangelist was Christ himself. He selected Apostles ("men sent") to proclaim his message of salvation *orally,* and this was perhaps done for as long as twenty-five years before the Gospel was set down in writing. There were, in fact, several classes of oral evangelists in the primitive Church (cf. e.g. Eph 4, 11).

This obviously means that the Church antedates the written Gospels and that they sprang from her bosom, for the Church is one with Christ, being nothing else than the incorporation of all authentic believers into his very own Body.

We have no New Testament evidence that Christ commanded his Apostles (or anyone) to write, just as we have no record that

Christ himself wrote anything other than some mysterious words
(?) in the sand when he was insidiously questioned about the
punishment due to an adulterous woman (Jn 7, 53—8, 11). In
the New Testament, as in the Old, it was the *oral transmission*
of the message that nearly always preceded any written form of
it, and this only accentuates the *living* character of the message.
Could you imagine St. Paul handing someone a book (even if
books had been abundant) when he was asked about the Christian faith? Paul would have *told* the questioner about the faith.
He was a "herald," and a herald cries out the message entrusted
to him.

Writing, as grateful as we are for it, was a secondary means
of proclamation. Paul wrote when he could not be on the spot
to proclaim the Good News, to answer questions, to settle disputes, or to put across a point. His writings (even allowing for
losses) are percentage-wise very small when compared with his
constant and zealous proclamation of the Message of the Gospel
of salvation: "Woe to me if I preach not the Gospel" (1 Cor
9, 16).

It is likely that the primitive heralding (kerygma) of the
joyous tidings of salvation had a certain common form. Our best
samples of this are found in the Acts of the Apostles, where Luke
has recorded (undoubtedly in a very abbreviated form) certain
primitive Gospel proclamations. We find one such kerygma in
Acts 10, 34–43, where Peter speaks to the Gentiles of good will
in Caesarea at the house of Cornelius: "I see clearly enough,
he said, that God makes no distinction between man and man;
he welcomes anybody, whatever his race, who fears him and
does what piety demands. God has sent his word to the sons
of Israel, giving them news of peace through Jesus Christ, who
is Lord of all. You have heard the story, a story which ran
through the whole of Judaea, though it began in Galilee, after
the baptism which John proclaimed; about Jesus of Nazareth,
how God anointed him with the Holy Spirit and with power,

so that he went about doing good, and curing all those who were under the devil's tyranny, with God at his side. We are witnesses of all he did in the country of the Jews, and in Jerusalem. And they killed him, hanging him on a gibbet; but on the third day God raised him up again, and granted the clear sight of him, not to the people at large, but to us, the witnesses whom God had appointed beforehand; we ate and drank in his company after his rising from the dead. And he gave us a commission to preach to the people, and to bear witness that he, and none other, has been chosen by God to judge the living and the dead. All the prophets bear him this testimony, that everyone who has faith in him is to find remission of sins through his name" (Knox).

We can hardly imagine that St. Peter said no more than this! Even a restless twentieth-century audience would not be content with so short a message. But this is the *substance* of the early kerygma, such as we find it expanded in St. Mark, who wrote down what Peter preached. The Acts are most helpful in getting at the most primitive oral Gospel, as preached to unbelievers or people not yet believers. Readers would profit immensely by paging through the Acts and noting some of the Gospel proclamations recorded there, such as that in 13, 16–41.

It is evident from studying the Acts that the earliest kerygma began with the work of John the Baptist and went as far as Christ's resurrection-ascension-enthronement. Included within these termini were something on his baptism, public life, signs and wonders, sayings, fulfillments, and his passion and death. The *Resurrection* was always given a place of honor, and the recent volume by F. X. Durrwell, C.Ss.R.[1], brings out in wondrous and competent manner the significance of this event.

It is hard to keep any message in a rigid form. Various circumstances, and differences in the Gospel heralds, soon brought on quite legitimate variations in the oral Gospel. Peter did not

[1] New York, Sheed & Ward, 1961.

preach in exactly the same way as Paul, nor Paul as John; and the needs of the newly formed Christian communities must have necessitated particular applications of the Good News to special cases. Too, there was always the question of heresy; deviation from correct doctrine. This had to be combatted, for it arose at a very early date and has never ceased to plague Christianity. All of these factors, and many others, brought on *variations* in the proclamation of the Gospel.

There was also the factor of the earliest liturgy, which had considerable to do with shaping the four Gospels as we now have them in the Bible. The nascent Christian community centered its life upon the Eucharist and the Word of God, and, as they "proclaimed the death of the Lord" (1 Cor 11, 26) through the Eucharist, they also proclaimed his Gospel and recounted the events that led up to his death and resurrection. This is one reason why the Passion narratives have such a remarkable sameness in all four canonical Gospels (although there are differences, of course). Numerous present-day scholars have also suggested that the baptismal formula in Mt 28, 19 is really the result of an early but developed liturgical formula, for baptism at first, according to Acts, was conferred only "in the name of Jesus" (Acts 10, 48; 19, 5). In this regard the address given by David M. Stanley, S.J., at the 1958 Liturgical Week, "Liturgical Influences on the Formation of the Four Gospels," might be read with the greatest profit.[2]

What we are really trying to say is that in order to *begin* to appreciate our four written Gospels we must take account of a lengthy and somewhat complicated oral history that led up to their final composition in the inspired form in which the Church now gives them to us.

Those who have attempted to follow the strong advice of St. Jerome, "never letting the Gospels depart from their hands," will

[2] Cf. *Proceedings*; or *Catholic Biblical Quarterly*, 21 (January, 1959), pp. 24–38.

have noted many unusual features about the four written Gospels. They will note that Matthew, Mark, Luke, and John, while being in *essential* agreement, present sayings, accounts, sequences of events, and details *with an amazing freedom of expression and liberty*. We need not think that it has taken twentieth-century scholars to discover this fact. It was noted very early in the Church. Already around 400 A.D. St. Augustine wrote a famous treatise "On the Agreement of the Evangelists." Gospel questions are largely summarized under two headings: the Synoptic Question and the Johannine Question.

Matthew, Mark, and Luke, since they have striking similarities and tend to view things together, are called "Synoptics" (from the Greek *syn-opto*, "to look at together"). This question is concerned with explaining how it is that these Gospels have so many similarities and yet so many differences—a "discordant concord." At times Gospel phrases will be verbatim the same; at other times the phrases are so different as to have a different meaning. The same may be said of incidents, ordering of materials, etc. We can best appreciate this if we use what is called a Gospel harmony or synopsis—an arrangement of the Gospels in parallel columns, thus facilitating comparisons.

John is a special case. His whole approach is different. A high percentage of his material is not found in the Synoptics—writing thirty or forty years after the others, he does not find it necessary to go over exactly the same ground once again. And his deeply spiritual presentation of, or penetration into, Sayings and events makes of him an evangelist apart—although on matters of fact he can be as accurate and detailed as any of them. Why does John write so differently? Is he setting out to give the remembered words of Christ? Or does he sometimes paraphrase and expand, bringing out meanings which it was by now clear the original words contained? May we sometimes find him going on from what Our Lord had said to his own

God-inspired reflection on them, e.g. Jn 3, 16–21? These are all facets of what is called the Johannine Question.

Both the Synoptic and Johannine Questions have been answered in many different ways. There is no final answer to either question, and the Church allows us to speculate *within certain boundaries.* Large volumes have been written on these matters, but they rarely succeed in rallying unanimous approval. The passage from oral to written Gospel, from Gospel to Gospels, is a thing so complicated and many-sided that we shall probably never arrive at a final solution of all the questions connected with it.

Having been urged by the Holy See to study these (and many other) questions, present-day scholars have agreed on certain principles at least, and it may be helpful to mention one of them. Most agree, for example, that the evangelists were little concerned about the fact that they did not record a Saying or incident *exactly* as another evangelist did. Judaism and Christianity are *historical* religions, based on things that actually happened. But rigorous historiography is a rather recent discipline —and by applying rigorous historicism to the Gospels (and to the Bible as a whole) we create problems for ourselves. If the ancients were less concerned than we with precision in every detail, then we must be prepared to acknowledge this and not demand from them something they never intended to give us.

All through the inspired writings we find variant accounts of the same incident. And it is clear that the writers are primarily concerned with the essential significance of what happened, rather than with all the details of its happening. Pius XII's emphasis on the study of literary forms as they then were should help us to read the Gospels as they were written.

Of the written Gospels it is very likely that Matthew comes first—yet not in the form of the Gospel as we have it today. Our present Matthew is in Greek. But we know from Papias of Hierapolis that Matthew wrote in Aramaic, the common language of the Jews of Palestine in Our Lord's day. Papias says he wrote the *"logia"*—utterances, memoirs perhaps—of Christ. We have no copy of this document, which was probably written about 50 A.D.

Next in line was the Gospel according to Mark, composed between 65 and 70 A.D., based on Peter's preaching, and still bearing the marks of a primitive and oral kerygma. Mark shows how "the Incarnate Son of God, Jesus Christ, has, in His public life, His death and resurrection, realized His vocation as the Servant of God."[3] As we *now have them*, Mark is the earliest of the written Gospels.

The Gospel according to Luke, the first of a two-volume work (Acts being the second volume), was the product (around 70 A.D.) of an outstanding convert from the Gentile world— a man of serene character and graciousness of mind. Luke, it would seem, wished through his writings to introduce the Gentile world to the marvels of Christ, and desired nothing more than to present the Saviour in the most attractive manner. As "the scribe of Christ's meekness" (Dante), Luke stresses universality ("Good News . . . for the *entire* people" 2, 10–11), joy, prayer, humility, Christ's goodness to women, so often mistreated in the Near East.

Luke employs in the Gospel one of his favorite devices: travelling. He centers his entire Gospel presentation on Jerusalem, and throughout a large section of it (9, 15—18, 14) has Our Lord journeying towards the Holy City. Once arrived there, Luke mentions no return to Galilee as do Matthew and John. In the travel section mentioned above, Luke brings in some of his magnificent parables: the Good Samaritan, Prodigal Son, Pharisee and Publican, the Rich Man and Lazarus.

The Greek version of Matthew—the only one we now have

[3] D. M. Stanley, S.J., "The Gospel of St. Matthew" in *The New Testament Reading Guide, Pamphlets on New Testament Introduction* (Collegeville, Minn.; Liturgical Press).

—probably contains not only a translation of the Aramaic document already mentioned, but additional matter besides. The translator may well have drawn on Mark and Luke, just as they may have drawn on the Aramaic Matthew. There is a most skillful *grouping together* of materials that stand scattered here and there in the other Gospels (e.g. the Sermon on the Mount). In fact, most scholars are prepared to see in Matthew a faint replica of the Pentateuch—five books, each made up of a discourse and of various events, all showing how the Church is none other than the Kingdom of God among us, and how Christ has *fulfilled* the Old Testament's messianic hopes. He is the new Moses, teaching from the mountain (as at Sinai).

John (most ingeniously) builds his Gospel presentation around conflict. The Light comes into a world filled with darkness, but the darkness is generally unwilling to receive it. The tension becomes so pitched that the Light of the World is put to death—yet this is only to end in triumph. Nearly the entirety of John's thought is magnificently capsuled in the Prologue that we read at the end of each Eucharistic sacrifice. John was most probably written around the year 100 A.D.

From these scattered and sparse remarks we can see how varied is the presentation of the Good News on the part of each evangelist, and yet how much the same. There is absolutely no reason why we should preoccupy ourselves with working out false harmonizations among the Gospels when such harmonizations were the very thing the evangelists saw no point in trying to achieve. One of the real acquisitions of Gospel study is *highlighting* the special features of *each* evangelist. Each, like the great heralds they all are, wishes to bring out the greatness of Christ in some special manner. Christ is too great to be treated in an absolutely stereotyped way.

Only Matthew and Luke present what are called Infancy Narratives: accounts regarding the birth and childhood of Our Lord. Matthew works more from the aspect of Joseph.

He alone introduces the Magi. Luke deals with the birth of John the Baptist and the Divine Saviour more from the aspect of Our Lady, contrasting the advent of these two in an amazing series of parallels. There is an artistry in Luke's account that no careful reader can fail to see. Just as prevalent is an effort to set all of these events against an Old Testament background.

Those desirous of doing some solid Gospel study might take up the revised edition of Father Bruce Vawter's *Popular Explanation of the Four Gospels*[4] and *The New Testament Reading Guide,* cited above, which contains valuable material on the Gospels of Matthew, Mark, and Luke and on the Johannine writings. Also of great interest are Father Alexander Jones' article "Gospel and Gospels"[5] and Vincent O'Keefe, S.J.'s "Towards Understanding the Gospels."[6]

24 *THE ACTS OF THE APOSTLES*

THE SEQUEL and companion volume of St. Luke's Gospel presentation is known as the Acts of the Apostles. It relates the story of Christian beginnings (cf. Acts 1, 1–2 and Lk 1, 1–4) during some thirty years after the death of Christ. The term "acts" (*práxeis*) is a technical one denoting actions performed in an outstanding manner by people or nations, and was much in vogue in the Hellenistic world. The book we are going to treat does *not* tell of the deeds of *all* the Apostles, but only of

[4] Huntington, Ind.; Our Sunday Visitor, 1961.
[5] *Scripture,* 12 (July, 1960), pp. 65–74.
[6] *Catholic Biblical Quarterly,* 21 (April, 1959), pp. 171–89.

some of them. The term "Apostle," too, is used rather widely, including men like Philip the Evangelist, Paul the Apostle, and Barnabas.

The Greek commentator Theophylact observed: "The Gospels contain the actions of the Son, the Acts contain those of the All-Holy Spirit." This is a most interesting observation, for Acts, like Luke's first volume, stresses the action of the Holy Spirit, intervening, enlightening, working out the thorny *problems of universalism*—a most acute question in the early Church, even if we now find it well-settled in principle. Acts, like Luke, is addressed to Theophilus, a noble convert—but at the same time to all Gentiles and Christians of good will.

Just as the Gospel according to St. Luke has two principal parts, the first dealing with the Galilean ministry of the Saviour, the second comprising an extended journey of his to Jerusalem with all that happened there; so Acts has two principal parts: the first dealing with the affairs of the Church in and around Jerusalem, featuring St. Peter; the second dealing with the missionary travels of St. Paul, extending the power of the Gospel throughout the Roman Empire—finally taking it to Rome itself. Luke, as we saw earlier, is fond of a travel-type presentation, even though this may call for a certain artistry and rearrangement of materials. Acts is, in fact, a mosaic of various incidents and episodes, all serving to illustrate the *progress and growth* of Christianity.

Like most books of the Bible, Acts may be variously divided. The division we offer will give the reader some idea of its contents and progression of movement (and the book is meant to be *moving*).

There is an *Introduction* (1, 1–11), linking Acts to the Gospel and partially repeating information presented in Lk 24, 13–53. Acts 1, 8 is especially important, since it gives us the theme and key to the entire book: "You shall receive the power of the Holy Spirit coming upon you, and you shall be witnesses in

Jerusalem, and in all Judaea, and Samaria, and even unto the ends of the earth." Here is Acts in a nutshell: the story of Christianity's expansion in numbers, in territory, and in its gradual understanding of its own universal character.

The *first main section* (1, 11—5, 42) centers on the Jerusalem community. Matthias is brought into the Apostolic College to replace the apostate Judas and to serve (like the other Apostles) as a *witness of the resurrection,* ever the crowning feature of the salvific work of Christ. Readers might well take note of the great importance attributed to Christ's resurrection all through Acts. The resurrection (and this is the doctrine of the Angelic and Common Doctor, St. Thomas) is not merely a source of hope, a pledge of victory, a proof of Christ's divine commission —it is an *essential part of the work of redemption* (see Rom 4, 25, the Easter Preface, and *Summa Theologica,* 3, q. 56, a. 2).

Another big event in this section of Acts is the *first Christian Pentecost,* not the "birthday of the Church"—a trite and inexact statement given scant recognition by Pius XII in his encyclical on the Mystical Body—but the *confirmation day of the Church; its day of manifestation and proclamation.* Once the Holy Spirit came upon the infant Church, it was ready to *act,* to *testify,* to labor enthusiastically and heroically for the spread of the Good News of Salvation to all men. The thesis of 1, 8 is illustrated already in this section by—among other things —St. Peter's Pentecostal sermon in 2, 14ff.: "God, then, has raised up this man, Jesus, from the dead; we are all witnesses of it. And now, exalted at God's right hand, he has claimed from his Father his promise to bestow the Holy Spirit; and he has poured out that Spirit, as you can see and hear for yourselves. . . . Let it be known, then, beyond doubt, to all the house of Israel, that God has made him Master and Christ, this Jesus whom you crucified. . . . Save yourselves, he said, from this false-minded generation" (Knox).

This same section of Acts gives us a valuable picture of the primitive Christian community at Jerusalem—its daily life centered on the Eucharist, prayer, the Word of God (the Good News of Salvation), and lively fraternal charity—all being of one mind. As we go through this section we may hope to absorb something of the wonderful sincerity and fervor of these early Christians. St. Pius X liked to admonish us to "return to the sources." Here is a source to which we can return. "These occupied themselves continually with the apostles' teaching, their fellowship in the breaking of bread, and the fixed times of prayer. . . . All the faithful held together and shared all they had . . . and as they broke bread in this house or that, took their share of food with gladness and simplicity of heart, praising God, and winning favor with all the people" (2, 42. 44, 46–7, Knox).

The *second* section of Acts (chs. 6 to 12) gives us some idea of the Church's *first missions*. Deacons are appointed in Jerusalem as a means of settling a dispute that arose among the ethnic groups. One of these Deacons, Stephen, delivers a discourse that fires the anger of a hostile element among the Jews, resulting in his martyrdom and the consequent dispersal of Christians. But this had its good side, bringing on expansions and missionary endeavors. These enthusiastic Christians could not keep silence about their new-found faith. They loved it, built their lives on it, and had no intention of keeping it to themselves: "We cannot possibly give up speaking of the things we have seen and heard" (4, 20).

The work of Philip the Evangelist is offered as a *sample* of that zeal which marked the infant Church. Philip, with all the agility of a sprinter, overtakes a chariot heading south along the Gaza road, and sits alongside an unnamed official of the Ethiopian queen. The official was busily engaged in reading his Old Testament. Philip's eager question: "Do you understand what you are reading?" is matched by the humble response: "How can I, unless some man show me?" After this short ex-

change of thought, Philip explains the famous 53rd chapter of
Isaiah which the official was reading. The instruction was
soon over, and the man was baptized—taking back to Ethiopia
his new-found faith.

In this same section of Acts we meet the *conversion of St.
Paul*—a tremendous moment in Christian annals. Paul, the
enemy and detester of Christ, becomes his most ardent and
uncompromising Apostle, bearing his name everywhere. A
"vessel of election," he will only cease his activity when he is
cut down by the sword. Paul, also known as Saul (he probably
had a Jewish and Roman name), already appeared at the
time of Stephen's martyrdom—as one of those "who approved
of his murder." Now, conquered by Christ, who identifies himself with his members, Paul will go forth to carry the Good
News further than anyone else mentioned in Acts. Success—but
also great suffering—was henceforth to be his lot. For some
time Paul and Barnabas worked closely together; and it was
Barnabas who brought the suspected Paul into the good graces
of the Christian community. We can hardly wonder that Paul
was suspect after the harsh treatment he had dealt to Christians
in Jerusalem and outlying districts.

But what of Peter? He, too, was busy—spreading the faith
about Palestine, and getting a much better understanding of
the universalism of Christianity and its relationship to Judaism.
His vision at Joppa (marking an end of the dietary laws of
Judaism), his success in bringing the pagan Cornelius and his
family into the faith, and the vehemence with which the Spirit
swept down on these men whom God had chosen—all of this
was a source of amazement to the former Galilean fisherman.
Though his initiative was not understood by all (bringing non-
Jews into the Church without their being circumcized or going
through any other Jewish ceremonial), he met a huge adapta-
tion problem—and his solution of it would ultimately be that
adopted by the entire Church. Finally, this section takes us up

to Antioch, where a flourishing Christian community had arisen and where the name "Christian" was first used.

Section *three* of Acts deals with Paul's first missionary journey (13, 1—15, 35). Paul and Barnabas, together with Mark, set out on this first journey, going across the island to Cyprus and up into Asia Minor. Colorful events mark their path—even deification at Lystra! (14, 8ff.). They return only for a Council held at Jerusalem, perhaps in 48 or 49 A.D. The Council, though not ecumenical in any technical sense, took an important and official stand on the procedure of receiving Gentile converts into the Church. This resulted in the proclamation of Christian liberty—freedom from the shackles of the Law (especially as expounded by the Pharisees). Only four requirements were laid upon Gentile converts, and these were local and in part temporary—a means of working out a modus vivendi with Jewish converts: abstention from meat offered to idols (see 1 Cor 8, 1ff.); from blood; from anything strangled; and from fornication (or: illicit marriages). This Council marks a great step forward in the expansion and growth of the Church, for now she is in a position to bring within her men of all backgrounds. It may well be that Acts 15 combines the results of two separate discussions on Jewish-Gentile problems, for there is some disharmony within the chapter.

Section *four* (15, 36—19, 20) takes us out once more into the mission field with St. Paul. He now has a new collaborator in the person of Silas (and will later recruit Timothy). Paul had had a falling-out with Barnabas over Mark (15, 36ff.), and the two men decided not to work together any more. We might even venture the observation that Paul, despite his great qualities, was not the easiest of men to get along with. During part of this second journey (from Troas to Philippi) Luke himself was with Paul, as we can tell by the so-called "we sections," where the author of Acts identifies himself with the travellers. The second journey took Paul far afield, even over to Athens, down to Corinth, and then eastward again. Doubling back to Ephesus, he took with him Aquila and Priscilla, two convert Jews, man and wife, who were to remain steadfast in their loyalty to Paul.

At this juncture Paul travelled as far as Caesarea Palestine and may have gone to Jerusalem. He certainly returned once more to Antioch in Syria and was soon on the road for a third missionary journey (18, 23). Here Luke intervenes to describe for us one of the colorful figures of the early Church —a man who was to cause Paul some trouble (1 Cor 3, 4), but who was perhaps also a trusted friend. This was Apollos, a Jewish convert from Alexandria, "an eloquent man, powerful in his use of the Scriptures" (18, 24). It is the opinion of more than one outstanding Catholic scholar that Apollos was the inspired ghost-writer of the Epistle to the Hebrews—so different from the other Pauline writings as to be disqualified from the usual type of Pauline authorship.

After a long stay in Ephesus which terminated in a riot (over magical practices and Diana idols), Paul set out for Jerusalem, stopping at various places along the way.

This marks the *fifth* section of Acts (19, 21—28, 29). Paul, now having covered a lot of the old ground, revisiting his churches, encouraging them, stabilizing them, ironing out their problems, moves on restlessly towards Jerusalem once more. However, the reader may infer that Paul is coming to a crisis in his life, especially when the Christian prophet Agabus (21, 10ff.) takes Paul's belt at Caesarea, binds his own hands and feet with it, and says: "Thus will the Jews in Jerusalem bind the man to whom this belt belongs, and hand him over to the Gentiles." And so it came to pass. Paul was arrested in Jerusalem after being warned how others felt about him—Jewish converts and Jews in general. After a long-drawn-out process he was sent to Rome for trial.

Paul's sea voyage to Rome, called by the critic E. Meyer

"a shining piece of factual correctness," is well told by Luke, Paul's companion. When Paul reaches Rome, via Cyprus and Malta, after many vicissitudes, the *Good News* also reaches "the ends of the earth," and Luke is content to terminate his second volume rather abruptly.

The historical reliability of Acts was at one time seriously questioned by men such as F. Ch. Baur (1845), but was restored to considerable honor by the even greater critic, Adolf von Harnack (1896). Whatever damage this latter scholar may have done in other fields of study, he turned the tide in the debate over Acts.

We should recall, nonetheless, that like all parts of the Bible, Acts is not a history book in the ordinary sense of the word. It is a profoundly religious document, "a history of early Christianity bathed in theology."[1] There is always danger when a piece of writing is forced into a literary category into which it was never intended to fit. Though amazingly reliable, even in some fine details, Acts is not history for history's sake. The remark of Sir William Ramsay bears repetition: "You may press the words of Luke in a degree beyond any other historian's, and they stand the keenest scrutiny and the hardest treatment, *provided always that the critic knows the subject* and does not go beyond the limits of science and of *justice*."[2] The theological values of Acts will always outweigh historical values. This is simply a consequence of the reasons for Luke's writing the account. Luke, in fact, is so faithful to his documentation that he will even reproduce in speech the orator's inexactitudes, as he does in Acts 7, 16.

In giving us the Acts, Luke (no other person has ever been seriously suggested as author) has made a tremendous con-

[1] C. P. M. Jones, "The Epistle to the Hebrews and the Lucan Writings" in *Mélanges R. H. Lightfoot*, pp. 113–43.

[2] *The Bearing of Recent Discovery on the Trustworthiness of the New Testament* (London, Hodder and Stoughton, 1915), p. 89.

tribution to our knowledge of the early Church—its *doctrine* (especially rich in this regard), its spirit, its trials, its expansion, and its guidance by the Holy Spirit.

Written after the Gospel, somewhere close to the year 70, Acts uses a vocabulary of about 2,000 words, around 450 of them being proper to this book. It includes 18 discourses (about one-fourth the book)—a common practice in classical Greek historiography.

In the Acts we find a freshness and simplicity that deserve our most sincere study and meditation, as well as our efforts to absorb its spirit. Here is first fervor at its best.

For additional reading we recommend Father Neal M. Flanagan's text and commentary in *The New Testament Reading Guide* and Robert-Tricot's *Guide to the Bible*.[3]

25 ST. PAUL AND HIS MESSAGE TO THE GENTILES

HUNDREDS OF BOOKS have been written on the life, epistles, travels, and especially the theology of St. Paul. Long years of study went into such works as Prat's famous *Theology of St. Paul*, or Bover's 956-page Spanish volume with the same title (not translated into English), or the dense and imaginative biography written in neo-Hebrew by the Jewish scholar Sholem Asch and translated into a number of languages, including English.

There will never be an end to such studies—whatever be

[3] Pp. 537–42.

their reliability or lack of it—for the simple reason that St. Paul was so profound a theological genius, so great a literary master, and so accomplished an organizer, thinker, and mystic (and many more things besides), that no one will ever succeed in fully explaining his thought or in completely exploring his Christ-centered personality.

When we say that St. Paul was a literary master, let us recall that he was tri-lingual, knowing and using Hebrew, Aramaic, and Greek; that the inspired writings he has left us were nearly all dictated to scribes, perhaps at times very rapidly; that he had to coin many words and attribute fresh and powerful meanings to others in order to get vehicles for his rich theological concepts; that there are even grammatical faults in his epistles, such as unfinished sentences, for Paul's ideas tumbled forth in such torrents that he could not always keep up with them or develop one line of thought before the urgency of another demanded his attention. Yet, despite these obstacles, the writings of St. Paul, even when presented in defective translation, have a power about them that is nearly irresistible.

Born somewhere around 5 A.D. in the flourishing Cilician town of Tarsus, Paul grew up in this cosmopolitan center, reared as a Pharisee by devout Jewish parents who traced their origin to the tribe of Benjamin and named their son after one of its great men, Saul. Saul (known also as Paul, a Roman type of name), was given a rabbinical education in Jerusalem under the famous Gamaliel, perhaps between the years of 20 and 25 A.D.

Around the year 35 A.D., while on his way to persecute Christians in Damascus—the world's oldest continually inhabited city—Paul was suddenly and miraculously converted to Christ. The event had a shattering effect upon Paul and dominated his entire subsequent life. The nineteenth-century efforts to explain this experience away as some kind of hallucination have long since ceased to be popular or acceptable in the scholarly world. Somewhere around 43 A.D., after years of reflection and spiritual ripening, Paul began his work as *herald* of the "inexhaustible riches of Christ," and this work he did not abandon until he fell as a martyr in Rome around the year 67.

Paul was never one to do things by halves. He committed himself wholly to any cause that he embraced, whether it was Pharisaism, persecution of Christians, or finally the Christian apostolate. His biographers love to describe his complicated and many-sided character. Though chronically ill (the nature of his illness has long been debated), he had an energy and drive that would put most men to shame; though physically weak, he spoke and acted mightily and took an interest in athletics and soldiery. Though nervous and restless, he never ceased thinking on a large scale, combining loyalty to traditions with an amazing originality of outlook.

He has been described as extremely bald, yet having big bushy eyebrows, out from under which peered sharp beady eyes; his stature was small, and his legs were bowed—not exactly a comely picture. Yet this energetic little man left no one around him listless. One had either to side with him or against him—as with Christ. He set every group on fire—whether with or against him—and as a herald of the good news he regarded himself as second to none, yet not through his own merits, but through the grace of God that drove him on and gave him no rest.

More than half of Paul's life was spent preaching Christ—and we should think of him first and foremost as a preacher. Paul even spoke of "his Gospel," for his doctrine was in agreement with that of the other Apostles (and *a fortiori* with that of Christ); also, he had been introduced to Christ in a special manner—to a Christ who is *one with his members*—and he had received special revelations to supply whatever might be wanting to his apostolic formation. As Paul advanced in years, he penetrated ever more deeply the meaning of Christianity.

Though he was certainly an original thinker and fell under the suspicion of other Apostles from time to time, his doctrine was in fact thoroughly in harmony with that of the other apostles, and all efforts to build up the case for a Pauline-Petrine opposition have failed.

Our knowledge of Paul comes almost exclusively from the Acts of the Apostles and from his own writings. Yet these writings, even allowing for the loss of some epistles, are quantitatively small when compared to the oral output of "the Apostle." Confining his efforts primarily to the Gentiles, Paul tackled a wide variety of practical and theoretical Christian problems, throwing himself into this endeavor in no detached manner. He became—what many moderns dread so much—*involved* and thoroughly wrapped up in everything and anything Christian; and the solution to every problem was ultimately Christ. Here was a man whom Christ had "overtaken" (Phil 3, 12) and whose whole life "was Christ" (Phil 1, 21).

To appreciate Paul's writings to the highest degree, we might recall that they were in many cases written to meet crises in the various Christian communities (usually ones that *he had founded*); that often these epistles (or letters) were first of all read by the communities to which they were directed, and that hence they can be most profitably read, even today, by a group, then discussed, reread, and pondered—as they undoubtedly were when first received.

Since it is absolutely unthinkable that a man of Paul's mental vigor remained static in his understanding and exposition of the Christian mysteries, we may expect to profit more from his writings by reading them *in chronological order*—as nearly as this can be determined. The order in which our Bibles present them is based (1) on their length and importance; (2) on community-letters being placed before individual-letters; and (3) on those of doubtful Pauline authorship being placed last, viz. the Epistle to the Hebrews, discussion on the authorship of which dates far back into Christian history.

St. Paul became, through the Will of God, the Apostle of the Gentiles; and though he made a number of attempts to offer the Christian message to Jewish groups, he was primarily concerned with the Gentiles (Gal 2, 8). The same may be said for his writings. The audience that he usually and primarily has in mind is a Gentile group. Let us run through his writings to get some idea of their contents—especially Paul's message to the Gentiles—and their approximate chronological order.

From Corinth, about the year 51–52, during his second missionary journey, Paul wrote his first letters to the *Thessalonians*. These two letters, probably the oldest writings of the New Testament, are centered on the great theme of *Christian hope*. Paul asserts that Christ, who has risen from the dead, who has accomplished our redemption, will *come again* (a doctrine known technically as the "Parousía"). This doctrine had a much greater place in the earlier Christian communities than it has today—and quite understandably. After nearly two thousand years of waiting, the matter does not have the urgency about it that it had for the primitive Christian community. In Thessalonica this doctrine had created several problems, for some gave up their jobs, thinking that the Parousía would occur very soon; others became unduly excited and alarmed; others considered it a disadvantage to die before the Parousía.

Whatever misunderstandings arose through his original preaching, or remained after the first letter had been received, were cleared up by the second letter to the Thessalonians. It is here that Paul asserts his ignorance of the precise time of Christ's Second Coming—a reserve that might well have been emulated by many excessively date-minded Christians throughout the history of the Church.

Eschatology, the study of the "last things," is an extremely complex subject, on the details of which Catholic scholars are not agreed. For Paul, at all events, Christ's resurrection had ushered in the "last days," the final phase of the divine plan. Going through the Thessalonians, the reader is made aware of the great place that *hope* has in the Christian life.

Though its date is much debated, as are also its precise recipients, the epistle to the *Galatians* is an extremely important document. It deals with the burning question of the relationship of the Mosaic Law to Christianity. In this letter, Paul refutes—not without strong language—the "Judaizers": those who expected Christians to be circumcized, to follow the Mosaic laws and observances, etc. For Paul the Mosaic Law has been abrogated; salvation is achieved through *faith* in Christ, not through any works of the Mosaic Law. What do the Galatians choose: liberty or enslavement? This short epistle is something of a rough sketch of the doctrine contained in that sent to the Romans later on.

The *Corinthians* were Paul's chief trouble-makers—his problem children. Yet Paul loved them, for they had made an heroic break with the scandalous life for which their town was widely known. Everyone knew what it meant "to live like a Corinthian" —expressed by a single verb in the Greek language: *korinthiázesthai.* Paul even called these converts "the letter we carry about with us, written in our hearts" (2 Cor 3, 2). It was from Ephesus that Paul wrote to them in the spring of 57 in order to settle a number of practical and speculative problems that had arisen among them. There is no other letter that so takes us into the *everyday life of the early Christian communities.* It deals with a host of matters: the notion of wisdom; cliques and parties within the community; the place of the human body in the Christian life; the ideals of Christian virginity and marriage; the problem of eating meat that had been offered to idols and was then set up for sale in the butcher shops; the question of veils for women; the celebration of the Eucharist and the liturgical assemblies; the value of the charismatic gifts of prophecy and tongues in relationship to charity (it was the abuse of the charisms that led Paul into his magnificent treatise on charity in 1 Cor 13); the question of the resurrection of the body from the dead, etc. We can be grateful, in one sense, that these questions arose among Christians of Corinth while Paul was *away* from the community, for otherwise we might lack the marvellous written treatment of them that we now have.

The second letter to the Corinthians was probably written in the fall of the same year. Here Paul bares his heart and his inner feelings as nowhere else—a man of remarkable sensitiveness. He also takes up the matter of a collection that he wants to send to the mother church in Jerusalem. Of Paul's "money-raising" methods, Msgr. Ronald Knox acutely observed that "he could wrap it up" much more skillfully than we moderns! Never did anyone treat the money question with greater delicacy than Paul.

From Corinth, perhaps in the winter of 57–58, Paul directed to the community of Rome (a church which he had not founded but which he hoped to visit soon) what we might regard as his most profound epistle. This epistle, which is well-ordered and marked by great doctrinal depth, is more of an *exposition* than anything else. It may have had the secondary purposes of refuting Judaizers and pacifying the discordant Jewish-Gentile elements in the Roman community, but it is primarily a development of a thesis stated in 1, 16–17: "I am not ashamed of the Gospel: for it is the power of God for the salvation of every believer, of Jew first and of Gentile. For the justice of God is revealed in it, beginning with faith and ending with faith, as it stands written: 'The just man lives by faith.'" Paul was no enemy of good works, as the moral exhortations in nearly every one of his epistles show; but he did strongly maintain that *at the moment* of justification, it was faith in Christ, and not the works of the Mosaic law code, that counted.

St. Paul wrote four epistles that are classified as the *Captivity epistles,* since they were written during some captivity. The question is, which captivity? Paul was a captive at least twice and probably several times. Many scholars believe that these four epistles,Colossians, Ephesians, Philippians, and Philemon, were written between 61 and 63. *Colossians* is a warning against the peculiar doctrinal errors prevalent in western Asia Minor —always a seed-bed of weird religious beliefs. Christ is superior to all created things, even angels—and nothing must be set before him.

Ephesians, which has great affinities to Colossians, deals with the Church as the Body of Christ. We are saved through incorporation into Christ, forming one Body with Christ. (Paul never uses the term "mystical" before Body.)

Philippians is something like "a conversation of a father with his very dear children," and is for the most part filled with joy. This community was Paul's greatest consolation, though there seem to have been some minor quarrels among its members. Phil 2, 5–11 is one of the most valuable Christological texts in all of Paul's writings.

Philemon has the unusual purpose of begging that a rich Christian master receive back his runaway slave, Onesimus, who, in the meantime, had become one of Paul's converts.

Three of Paul's writings are known as the *Pastoral Epistles,* viz. 1 and 2 Timothy, and Titus. They have a close relationship and were perhaps written between 65 and 67. Though not giving anything like a complete list of pastoral duties, they do offer a valuable collection of pastoral hints together with some important doctrinal information on the formation of the hierarchy within the primitive Church. The Second Epistle to Timothy is a touching farewell letter from Paul to his beloved son and co-worker.

The *Epistle to the Hebrews* is a magnificent treatise on the superiority of the Christian over the Levitical priesthood; of Christ over Moses; of the New Law over the Old Law; of Christ's sacrifice over the sacrifices of the New Testament. All of this is put into the form of an exhortation—for a group of converts who are obviously undergoing a trial. Yet we cannot say when the letter was written; or to whom it is addressed (a group of convert Jewish priests in Palestine has been suggested); or to what extent Paul is the author of the epistle. The Biblical Commission on June 24th, 1914, allowed considerable latitude in the matter of Paul's authorship, and Catholic authors have not failed to avail themselves of this directive, most of them regarding Paul as no more than the guiding spirit behind the epistle, allowing considerable latitude to his scribe. Père M.-J. Lagrange, O.P., thought that the epistle was certainly written before the catastrophe of 70 A.D., for the Jewish institutions are spoken of as still being carried on.

Scholars are, of course, busy re-examining, and going ever deeper into, the doctrine of St. Paul. We might mention specifically the doctrinal significance of the resurrection and the basic meaning of the term "Body of Christ." Canon Cerfaux of Louvain, Père Benoit of Jerusalem, Père Lyonnet of the Roman Pontifical Biblical Institute, and our own American scholar Barnabas M. Ahern, C.P., have all made valuable contributions towards an ever deeper understanding of Paul's "Body" doctrine, in keeping with the request of Pope Pius XII in his 1943 encyclical on the subject.

We have only touched on many facets of Paulinism. Readers who wish some good material might take up the excellent little volume of Amédee Brunot, S.C.J., *St. Paul and His Message;*[1] *The Resurrection*, by F. X. Durrwell, C. Ss. R.; the still valuable

[1] New York, Hawthorne, 1960.

(though slightly dated) *Theology of St. Paul,* by Ferdinand Prat, S.J.;[2] the *New Testament Reading Guide;*[3] or the fine little volume of Henri Daniel-Rops, *St. Paul, Apostle of the Nations.*[4]

26 *THE APOCALYPSE: VISION OF CHRISTIAN VICTORY*

IF THERE IS any book within the inspired biblical library that merits the name of "mystery book" it is surely the Apocalypse. St. Jerome stated, though with considerable exaggeration, that it contains "as many mysteries as words." This, however, should not frighten us away from the book. As a matter of fact, the primary purpose for which the Apocalypse was written was *not* to frighten its readers. The author wished to correct abuses, as a cursory reading of the letters to the seven churches in chapters 2—3 will quickly show; but more than that, he wished to *console* and *fortify* his readers, for they were about to undergo heavy persecution and were, consequently, in need of encouragement and hope. The Apocalypse is a victory book, heralding the victory of Christ, who, with his members (his bride, 21, 2ff.), will triumph over all obstacles, no matter how great. His victory was assured from the first, but it is worked out through the entire history of the Church and will blossom forth in full glory only at the end: "He who is victorious—I will make him a pillar in the temple of my God; he shall never

---

[2] Westminster, Newman, 1946.
[3] Nos. 5–11.
[4] Chicago, Fides, 1951.

leave it. And I will write the name of my God upon him, and the name of the city of my God, that new Jerusalem which is coming down out of heaven from my God, and my own new name" (3, 12).

Readers are likely to think that the Apocalypse is a unique piece of writing, that it is the only thing of its kind. This is far from true. In the pre-Christian centuries and for some two centuries after Christ, the "apocalyptic" was a *standard type* of literature, exemplified countless times both within and outside the Bible. The apocalyptic literary form is present (among other places) in Is 24—27; here and there in Ezekiel; in Dan 7—12 (especially); in Joel; in Zechariah 9—14; in Mt 24 (and parallels in Mark and Luke) and 2 Pet 3 within the Bible; and there are any number of apocalypses among the apocryphal (noncanonical) writings, e.g. book of Enoch; Apocalypse of Moses; book of Jubilees; Assumption of Moses; Apocalypse of Baruch; and Apocalypse of Abraham. The "apocalypse" was a well-known type of literature with rules of its own, just as we have in our own times the language of sports, or that of the beatniks. The apocalypse sets out to convey some important "revelation" or "unveiling" (such is the meaning of the Greek word) of facts hidden or known to God alone, some vision of the present or future, conveyed in grandiose or cosmic terminology, using numbers that had an interpretative value, frequently not so much saying things about the future as seeing a deeper significance in present events—at times viewing them *as if* from the past. While there were general rules of apocalyptic writing or speaking, there were also variations, and "apocalypses" differed in value and authenticity. To view our canonical Apocalypse without any reference to what we have come to learn about the literary form of "apocalypse" would be to leave ourselves open to misinterpretation. To state that "there is no evidence that the Beloved Disciple planned the book, and every internal reason to believe the plan divine"[1] is to ignore the language that is common to this type of writing. The "revelation" that our Apocalypse makes—and that, most successfully and forcefully—is simply this: Christ, with his members, is the Victor. He (the slain, yet glorified and *standing* Lamb) conquered death; and he will conquer every other obstacle; and those who adhere to him in sincerity and loyalty will share in his victory. The Apocalypse *in this sense* is an unfolding of the future; but it is not the prediction of various isolated events (such as the Protestant Reformation, the Nazi movement, etc.), and all efforts at such interpretation have ended in failure.

What we would like to make clear is this: our Apocalypse is the most successful and dignified of all apocalypses; it is the *expression* of a message (*not* necessarily received in the apocalyptic form) that its author had truly received from God.

Our Apocalypse, according to its opening verses, comes from God, is passed on to the Son, is given to an angel, is communicated through John (on the Island of Patmos) to the seven (i.e. representing *all*) churches of Asia Minor, and through them to the entire Christian world of all places and times. The Apocalypse has a *tremendous value for us today,* since we fall within its audience of reader-hearers as much as the author's contemporaries. The Christian life is not intended to be easy; and Christians need encouragement. We need warnings, too; and the Apocalypse offers both.

The whole Christian era, from the Coming of Christ on, is regarded by the New Testament writers as the "last times" (1 Cor 10, 11). There is an urgency, a sense of destiny, of importance, of great decision, that constantly runs through Christian history, and we find precisely this in the Apocalypse. Here is a Christian philosophy of history, a demonstration that

---

[1] James M. Culleton, *A Key to the Apocalypse* (Fresno, Cal., Academy Guild Press, 1959). This work is in general unreliable. See *Catholic Biblical Quarterly* 21 (July, 1959), pp. 404–5.

God, through his Redeemer Son, rules all the courses of men, even when it looks very much as if "God is writing straight with crooked lines."

It is a pity that the Apocalypse has been regarded as a kind of "horror book," serving fanatical sects as a means of stirring up unrest, and used as an aid in setting dates relative to the "end of the world." To use the symbolic numbers of the Apocalypse (1000 = a multitude; 12 = the Church as the New Israel; 7 = perfection or plenitude; 3½, as half of seven, = time of combat, with its month-multiple, 42, and its day-multiple 1260, having the same connotation)—numbers which had a fixed meaning—as a means of setting dates is about as far from the true purpose and significance of the Apocalypse as one can get. Every so often we encounter a new "dating-system," this time foolproof, relative to the "end of the world," often enough founded upon the Apocalypse. All of these systems have so far failed. Only those that put themselves rather confortably far out in the remote future can enjoy a little glory until time proves them false.

The Apocalypse is not an easy book. It found its way into the New Testament Canon only with difficulty. The Eastern Church especially was reluctant to grant it admission (largely because of its use by heretics). St. Cyril of Jerusalem and St. Gregory of Nazianzus, both of them doctors of the Church, formally excluded it from their canonical listings (at that time the Canon of Scripture had not been defined). The Syrian Church never gave this book a place in its famous translation of the Bible known as the Peshitto. Yet the Western Church showed the Apocalypse more favor, and as time went on Eastern opposition weakened. The Apocalypse, though still called a "deutero-canonical book" (i.e. one that was admitted to the Canon only with difficulty), is as much a part of our Bible as any other book that is found there.

We might think that the Apocalypse, since it is placed last

in the Bible, was written last of all the New Testament books; just as we are inclined to think the same thing, conversely, about Genesis. Neither assumption is correct. The Apocalypse, nonetheless, is well placed where it is, since it does reach out into the future of the Church. Actually it was written between 94 and 96, a few years *before* the writing of the Gospel according to John.

The Greek of the Apocalypse is about the poorest that we find in the New Testament—much poorer than that of the Fourth Gospel and quite different in style, vocabulary, and thought, too. It has never been unanimously admitted that John the Evangelist wrote both books, at least in the same way. If he wrote both of them, he must have used a better scribe for the Gospel, and either a poorer one or none at all for the Apocalypse. The Church has never made any pronouncement on the Johannine authorship of our book, nor is the question as important as some might think.

The plan of the Apocalypse has been very carefully studied by scholars. At times brilliant men have thought that they had worked out a perfect plan, consisting of seven septenaries, only to have other scholars come along and point out flaws in their explanation. Too, the theory has been advanced by Père M. E. Boismard, O.P.,[2] and has met with considerable favor, that the Apocalypse consists of a fusion of what were once two separate apocalypses!

Leaving aside more detailed divisions of the book, we may point out that, aside from the introduction (s) and the epilogue, the book has two principal but unequal divisions: 1, 9—3, 22, revolving around the seven representative churches of Asia Minor; and 4, 1—22, 5, presenting the vision proper. It is in this latter part of the Apocalypse, by far the most complicated, that we find such varied subjects and symbols as the heavenly

[2] *L'Apocalypse*[3]: La Sainte Bible, traduite en français sous la direction de l'Ecole Biblique de Jerusalem (Paris, Editions du Cerf, 1959).

throne; the twenty-four elders; the four living creatures; the
Slain Lamb; the Sealed Book; the four Horsemen; many angels;
the Elect in heaven; the seven Trumpets; the two Witnesses;
the Woman and the Dragon; the seven-headed and ten-horned
Beast; the False Prophet; the friends of the Lamb; the Harvest
of the Nations; the seven Bowls (Vials); the Fall of Babylon;
the Harlot and the Beast; final Battles; and the heavenly Jerusalem. As a mere leafing through the book will reveal, this is a
serious matter. On the other hand, there are constant messages
of victory scattered throughout the book, and it closes on a
note of optimism: "Happy are those who wash their robes
clean! They have the right to the tree of life and will enter by
the gates of the city. . . . Come, Lord Jesus! The grace of the
Lord Jesus be with you all" (22, 14. 21).

One feature that will soon come to the notice of an alert
reader of the Apocalypse is its heavy, almost constant, use of
the *Old Testament*. The author knew the Old Testament well
and pressed into service image after image that he found in it,
showing preference for such books as Genesis, Exodus, Psalms,
Isaiah, Ezekiel, Daniel, Zechariah and Joel. The Apocalypse
contains an unusually large proportion of Old Testament citations and/or allusions—in fact, it is a mosaic work of Old Testament borrowing.

Learned men have racked their brains from the earliest
Christian centuries, trying to figure out a system for interpreting
the Apocalypse. Nothing definite has ever been decided upon.
Systems have ranged all the way from concentration on the
contemporary scene to strictly eschatological (end-time) in-
terpretations. Others have seen the entire history of the Church
portrayed in the Apocalypse, and this in varying ways, viz.:
(a) successive periods of the Church (even references to precise
historical events); (b) various tabloids, *each* of which refers to
the entire history of the church—not to successive periods; or (c)
the entire book describes in a general manner the history of the

Church—contemporary, future (in any sense) and end-time. These systems have been given technical names, mostly German (such as *zeitgeschichtlich*), with which it is useless to burden our readers. For practical purposes, we are safe if we read the Apocalypse as a depiction of the *entire general* history of the Church, written from the standpoint of first-century Asia Minor, and aimed at showing that all persecutions, all trials, and all sorrows, if borne with and in Christ, will lead the Christian to victory with Christ, the Invincible Conqueror.

The Church has said practically nothing about this book, other than defining its canonicity (Council of Trent) and making a decision in 1944 through the Holy Office about one "unsafe" method of interpreting the millennium (1,000 years) of chapter 20.

Are there any startling developments in the study of the Apocalypse today? Yes and no. This is not a book that will be illuminated by archaeological discoveries—though the discovery of *more* literature of this class (of which we already have *much*) might possibly throw additional light on its interpretation. The two major contributions by Catholics have both been made by Dominicans, E. B. Allo, who has written one of the really great and timeless commentaries on the book (1921);[3] and M. E. Boismard,[4] at present teaching at the Ecole Biblique in Jerusalem, and one of the most fertile thinkers in the New Testament field. The work of these men, the fruit of which is partially included in this chapter, is outstanding. There is little hope for anything like an absolutely unanimous interpretation of the Apocalypse.

This does not mean that the average reader cannot derive immense value from reading this book. It was meant for the average reader. It was intended to give him comfort, courage, consolation, warning, and hope. "The Apocalypse is the great

[3] *Saint Jean: l'Apocalypse*[3] (Paris, Gabalda, 1933).
[4] *Op. cit.*

epic of Christian hope, the triumphal song of the persecuted Church."[5]

Readers who want an inexpensive but highly valuable booklet (forty-four loaded pages) on the Apocalypse should purchase *Revelation, a Divine Message of Hope*, by Bruce Vawter.[6] It is a reliable guide. For those who read French, the work on the Apocalypse by H. M. Feret, O.P., is a valuable book. (I cannot recommend the English translation).

27 THE PLACE OF THE BIBLE IN CHRISTIAN LIFE

IN MANY WAYS this final chapter is the hardest one to write, first because I would like to leave the reader with something of an authentic Catholic attitude towards the Bible; and second because I would like this chapter to serve as a fitting conclusion to the work that has gone into what has already been written— often amidst many other pressing duties.

This book was written for several reasons. One of them is this: there is a good deal of bewilderment about "what is happening to our Bible." This bewilderment is not limited to the faithful. As a matter of fact, the study being expended upon the Bible at the present time is so vast and intense and progressive that even those who are supposed to be scholars in the field

[5] *Ibid.*

[6] Knights of Columbus Pamphlet Series No. 51; available from The Knights of Columbus Religious Information Bureau, 4422 Lindell Blvd., St. Louis 8, Missouri.

have to devote long hours of study to Sacred Scripture and to what is being written about it if they wish to remain abreast of what is going on. There is no reason for disguising this fact, especially when it is explicitly dealt with in the 1950 *Instruction* of the Biblical Commission. To be a biblical scholar is a lot of work—even if it is one of the most sublime tasks that can be entrusted to man. Scholars themselves feel at times overwhelmed by the deluge of books, articles, and discoveries that come to their attention every day.

It is true, and you were given the word of Pius XII in confirmation of the fact, that "the conditions of biblical studies . . . have greatly changed within the last fifty years." We have seen the reasons for this. We have also seen that there is no serious cause for alarm or fright. A tremendous amount has been learned about the Bible in the past hundred years—more so than at any other period in the history of the Church. This, however, does not mean that the Bible has changed. The Bible is today what it has always been from the time that it was finally gathered together to form the sacred library that it is: it is the inspired, formally inerrant, Word of God, written down by men who functioned as "living and reasonable instruments" of God, the principal author; and its purpose is to acquaint us with God's plan of salvation, to instruct us, to stir us up, and to lead us along the paths of eternal blessedness. *In no essential respect has the Bible changed, nor has the Church's attitude towards the Bible changed.* We must make this clear in order to obviate such exaggerated statements as "only scholars now dare to speak about the Bible" or "the whole Bible is now looked upon differently." Let us retain a balanced outlook, especially where "the most precious source of doctrine on faith and morals" (Pius XII) is concerned. It is our hope that what we have written will offer some reassurance that not everything has changed with regard to the Bible. We have purposely dealt with some of the more important issues—even those that are the most delicate—in order that you may understand the present-day position of the Church and of those whom she has entrusted with the study and exposition of her Sacred Books, always under her guidance.

The Bible is and always will be a *religious library*. This fact should remain foremost in our minds. Its purpose is not, therefore, to offer the same information in the same manner as we would expect to find it in non-sacred sources. Nearly everything in Sacred Scripture, even when it springs from a mentality and age that is less perfect than we like to think ours is, is *religious*.

Furthermore, in putting across the most varied religious lessons, the biblical writers made use of different types of writing (literary forms), such as: poetry; didactic fiction (many of our Lord's parables); apocalyptic; irony; polemic; epic; legislation; letter-style; oratory; emotional outbursts, and various forms of religious history (*none* of which is governed by the canons of modern historical writing, but which need not for that reason be unhistorical). It is especially in this matter of literary forms—so illuminating and helpful and at the same time so dangerous—that Pius XII has given very specific instructions. If we are to arrive at the basic *meaning* of Sacred Scripture, that is, its *literal sense*, we *must*, he says, determine the various types of writing which the biblical authors actually employed in setting down their inspired instruction.

For some reason, many come to the Bible with the notion that it contains only *one* type of writing, and that is *sober historical narrative*. Ancient oriental literature—and the Bible is oriental and ancient, the latest part of it being *at least* 1,850 years old—displayed as rich a variety of literary forms as any other literature, and *none of these forms*, said Pius XII, is to be excluded from the Bible *on principle* unless it "contradicts the holiness and truth of God." There is such a thing as being too "serious" about the Bible, failing to catch its subtle humor, which is no enemy of either holiness or truth but is rather often allied to both. In this regard the book of Jonah, to mention but one, has suffered horribly.

Similarly, many scholars have labored so seriously over the theological problem they thought they perceived in 1 Kgs 22, 20ff., failing to note the really clever irony of the prophet Micaiah, son of Imlah, that their explanations have "issued in solemn scholarly nonsense." Sometimes we may be a little too "historical" for our own good, and "history," as the Biblical Commission's 1948 letter to Cardinal Suhard so clearly states, is one of the areas where we need some *adjustment*. It was not without good reason that this letter laid upon scholars the delicate and difficult task of discovering what notion of "historical truth" the ancient orientals entertained.

Nearly everything that we have written has been intended to illustrate the directives given by the Holy See in the last twenty years, much of which *implicitly modifies former directives,* as was explicitly stated in writing by both the Secretary and the Sub-secretary of the Biblical Commission in 1955. Nor do we feel that the June 1961, "warning" of the Holy Office means to alter these principles, though it does expect a more prudent and accurate application of them.

It is, of course, important for Catholics to acquaint themselves with the recent developments in biblical research, whether these be the fruit of archaeological discovery, or philology, of literary analyses, of comparative religion, or some other branch of investigation. It has never been the mind of the Church to discourage serious study, even though not all have the ability or (especially) the energy to undertake such study. Sometimes the much-abused term "simple faith" is almost synonymous with sheer mental laziness.

People who do not really know their faith (or have enough interest to study it) easily fall prey to the arguments of unbelievers, and this is especially true where the Bible is concerned. St. Peter instructed the Christians of his day not only "to en-throne Christ as Lord in their hearts," but also "to be ready at all times to give an account of the hope which they cherish" (1 Pet 3, 15, Knox).

The fact, however, that we are asked to study the Bible scientifically—really to expend intelligent *effort* in getting at its meaning, through any and every aid that we can find—does not mean that we should or can ever cease to read the Bible *devoutly and religiously*. It would be a great mistake to limit our contacts with the Bible to those of an academic nature. *There are many ways to use the Bible.* Serious study is but one of them—though an indispensable one. Another way to use the Bible is meditation: the prayerful, devout, reflective reading of the inspired pages. The earliest monks and Fathers of the Church regarded the Bible as *the* meditation book. Nor would they ever have considered one reading of the Bible as sufficient. It must be read and meditated upon again and again, for, being inspired, it has a limitless, inexhaustible message to convey to us.

To become *familiar* with Sacred Scripture, one must read it regularly and often. It is only in this way that one gains the "feel" of the biblical mentality and makes it something of his own. This is an exercise fruitful for *all* Christians—priests, religious, and faithful alike. Abbot B. C. Butler of Downside recently stated: "It is part of our Christian conviction that to hear and respond to the Word of God is our single, all-embracing task here below; that without it our life is but an idiot's tale." For centuries Christians gained access (among other ways) to the Word of God by reading and meditating Scripture—allowing, of course, for the fact that oral instruction had such a predominant place in the primitive Church. But, along with this, the Scriptures were publicly read, often at considerable length, in the language of the people, and all listened. Those who had copies of Scripture, and who could read, supplemented this public reading by personal meditation. Pius XII has asked us to follow this practice—however rare it might be at the present moment.

The Church gives much time and honor to the inspired Scriptures in her official worship, and this is still another way in which we may use the Bible. Since a large portion of the Old Testament *arose through* liturgical use, and much of the New Testament was formed through and *destined for* liturgical use, we may naturally expect special fruits from the liturgical use of the Bible. This fact is being increasingly appreciated by both biblical and liturgical specialists. F. L. Moriarty, S.J., speaks of many of the Old Testament accounts as having been drawn up for liturgical usage as a means of "dynamic retention" of "salvation-history."[1] Father Roland E. Murphy, O.Carm., of the Catholic University of America, states that "the traditions concerning the events at Sinai doubtless had their origin in Israelite liturgy. . . . All the elements of this Israelite liturgy can be found in chapters 19—24 of Exodus. . . . These chapters give us a theological interpretation of these events as they were understood and *liturgically re-enacted* by the people of Israel."[2] There is no reason why the biblical and liturgical revivals should remain apart. They belong to one another.

The thought may occur to some that intellect and piety do not go hand in hand. Only a false definition of intellect and/or piety could produce such a preposterous conclusion. Intellectual *pride* will not foster genuine piety, and pietism has little regard for *any* use of the intellect. Some of the greatest biblical scholars of our times were men noted for their genuine and sincere piety, among them Père M.-J. Lagrange, O.P., founder of the Ecole Biblique in Jerusalem, and Abbé Joseph Chaine, of Lyons. While a spirit of carping criticism can undermine piety, a spirit of humble criticism and mental alertness cannot.

[1] *Op. cit.*
[2] *Book of Exodus, Text and Commentary* (New York, Paulist Press, 1960), Vol. II, p. 5.

In the program that Pius XII outlined in his 1943 encyclical, we, priests and faithful alike, should both be aware of the intellectual aspects of our faith and at the same time be sincerely devout. The blend may not be easy to achieve, but it is an authentic ideal and necessary for us as individuals and as members of the Church. St. Jerome bitterly complained in his day about devout but ignorant Christians—about the disservice that such people may render the Church by not being able to explain and defend their faith.

To all of us, no less than to Timothy, are St. Paul's words applicable: "All Scripture is divinely inspired and useful for giving instruction, for reproof, for correcting faults, and for training in uprightness; so that the man of God may be ready and equipped for every good work" (2 Tim 3, 16–17).

INDICES

INDEX TO SCRIPTURE TEXTS

Note. Standard English spellings have been used throughout this book with but few exceptions. The following list, with abbreviations, should clarify any misunderstanding with regard to the books of the Bible that have been cited or mentioned.

Genesis(Gen); Exodus(Exod); Leviticus(Lev); Numbers(Num); Deuteronomy(Dt); Joshua[Josue](Jos); Judges(Jdg); 1 and 2 Samuel[1 and 2 Kings](1 and 2 Sm); 1 and 2 Kings[3 and 4 Kings] (1 and 2 Kgs); 1 and 2 Maccabees (1 and 2 Macc); Job; Psalms(Ps); Qoheleth[Ecclesiastes](Qoh); Canticle of Canticles(Cant); Wisdom (Wis); Sirah[Ecclesiasticus or Sirach or Ben Sirah](Sir); Isaiah(Is); Jeremiah(Jer); Ezekiel(Ez); Daniel(Dan); Hosea[Osee](Hos); Amos; Obadiah[Abdias]; Jonah; Micah[Michaeus]; Habakkuk[Habacuc]; Zephaniah[Sophonias]; Haggai[Aggaeus]; Zechariah[Zacharias]; Malachi[Malachias]; Matthew(Mt); Mark(Mk); Luke(Lk); John (Jn); Acts; Romans(Rom); 1 and 2 Corinthians(1 and 2 Cor); Galatians(Gal); Ephesians(Eph); Philippians(Phil); Colossians(Col); 1 and 2 Thessalonians(1 and 2 Thess); 1 and 2 Timothy(1 and 2 Tim); Titus(Tit); Philemon; Hebrews(Heb); James(Jas); 1 and 2 Peter(1 and 2 Pet); 1, 2, 3 John(1, 2, 3 Jn); Jude, Apocalypse (Apoc).

¹ The Psalm enumerations are given according to the Hebrew text. This is usually one unit *above* the Vulgate enumeration. While both enumerations are frequently listed in the book, only the Hebrew enumeration is listed here.

INDEX OF NAMES AND TOPICS

MONAST